MARGARET   ESLIE

Theatre of Discord

Theatre of Discord
Dissonance in Beckett, Albee, and Pinter

Bob Mayberry

Rutherford ● Madison ● Teaneck
Fairleigh Dickinson University Press
London and Toronto: Associated University Presses

Associated University Presses
440 Forsgate Drive
Cranbury, NJ 08512

Associated University Presses
25 Sicilian Avenue
London WC1A 2QH, England

Associated University Presses
P.O. Box 488, Port Credit
Mississauga, Ontario
Canada L5G 4M2

Library of Congress Cataloging-in-Publication Data

Mayberry, Bob, 1950–
    Theatre of discord : dissonance in Beckett, Albee, and Pinter / Bob Mayberry.
      p. cm.
    Bibliography: p.
    Includes index.
    ISBN 0-8386-3353-6 (alk. paper)
    1. English drama—20th century—History and criticism.
    2. Cognitive dissonance in literature.   3. Theater of the absurd.
    4. Beckett, Samuel, 1906– —Criticism and interpretation.
    5. Albee, Edward, 1928– —Criticism and interpretation.
    6. Pinter, Harold, 1930– —Criticism and interpretation.
    I. Title.
PR739.C63M38   1989
822'.91'09—dc19   88-45786
                                                        CIP

Printed in the United States of America

For Kansas & LJ

Contents

Acknowledgments

I owe much to my friend and mentor, Don Kunz, University of Rhode Island, whose sense of humor made grad school enjoyable and whose encouragement still rings in my ears. The best teacher I have ever known.

To David Jones, University of Utah, a special thanks for his serendipitous suggestion that I do a seminar paper on language and light.

And to Deborah Mitchell for her sensitive editing; and June Schlueter, Lafayette College, for her generous evaluation and helpful suggestions, my gratitude.

Portions of this manuscript appeared in the following:

Edward Albee: Planned Wilderness, Patricia De La Fuente, ed., Living Author Series no. 3, Pan American University, 1980; and *Kansas Quarterly*, Harold Schneider, ed., 12, no. 4, (Fall 1980).

Theatre of Discord

1

A Theatre of Discord

"Art . . . is shaped by the way space is perceived."[1] Painting, sculpture, architecture, mime, and other visual arts are dominated by visual space, while music is shaped by acoustic space. Dramatic art, however, takes place at the intersection of visual and acoustic space. Theatre, Eugene Ionesco reminds us, "appeals as much to the eye as to the ear."[2]

Light and sound, then, provide both the grounds and the limits of theatrical performance. Visual space includes everything the audience sees—setting and lighting, costumes and makeup, gesture and movement—all of which are conveyed by the medium of light. Therefore, light is information-bearing; it defines space and conveys picture-messages to an audience. John Fletcher and John Spurling compare light on the stage to print on the page. "The *sine qua non* of a theatrical event," they write, "is light (or its absence)."[3]

On the other hand, acoustic space—what the audience hears—includes human and nonhuman sounds as well as silence. Although noise, music, and silent pauses are often used to create mood or underscore dialogue, language remains the preeminent medium of acoustic space. Like light, language bears information to an audience but is capable of both more complexity and more precision. Consequently, the Western stage has been dominated by the spoken word. In effect, the visual has served primarily as an extension of the verbal. For example, the importance placed on the history and psychology of character in realistic drama is physically manifested in costumes and settings that reinforce the relation between character and environment revealed and developed in dialogue. Traditionally, the messages conveyed to audiences by the twin media of drama, sight and sound, are complementary.

Of course, dialogue may on occasion be ironically opposed to the visual, as, for example, in *Waiting for Godot* where Estragon's last line, "Yes, let's go," is contradicted by the stage direction, "They do not move."[4] Although *Godot* is not usually described as traditional, it shares with realistic theatre a consonance of the visual and verbal. The irony of Estragon's final line is evident in the first place because the conventional harmony of sight and sound, which is the norm throughout the play, has been momentarily violated and therefore brought under scrutiny. The moment is startling because it is unusual. The audience expects the consonance of the visual and the verbal to be restored. The ironic tension generated between the seen and the heard is, in *Godot* as in traditional theatre, temporary.

To construct a play on the principle of dissonance, on the permanent rupture of light and language, constitutes a major break with a dramatic convention that assumes a nonproblematic conjunction of visual and verbal. Samuel Beckett, Edward Albee, and Harold Pinter have each experimented with the disassociation of acoustic and visual space in certain one-act plays: *Play* and *Breath* by Beckett, *Box* and *Quotations from Chairman Mao Tse-tung* by Albee, and *Landscape* and *Silence* by Pinter. Visual and verbal space are "filled" with different contents that create dissonance between the two media, light and language. The information transmitted to the audience by what they see is not synchronous with that communicated by what they hear. As a result, the traditional goals of unity and consonance within each work are replaced by fragmentation and dissonance. The center of dramatic action shifts away from the usual conflict between characters or the ideas they represent and relocates in the tension between the two simultaneous modes of audience perception, which are also the modes of performance production.

What these one-act plays offer the spectator, then, are two simultaneous but disassociated performances—one seen, the other heard. The separation of the visual and verbal media violates the usually indestructible bond of language and action. It creates a series of verbal and visual nonsequiturs that surprise and frustrate an audience whose expectation—that consonance will be restored by play's end—has been conditioned by the conventions of realistic theatre. As a consequence of the lack of harmony between sight and sound, spectators experience cognitive dissonance, the psychological tension resulting from the incompatibility of contiguous stimuli. Once aware of the inconsistent messages received from what they hear and what they see, the spectators feel pressured to resolve the dissonance. "The strength of the pressure to reduce dissonance," explains psychologist Leon Festinger, "is a function of the magnitude of the existing dissonance."[5] Cognitive dissonance, then, functions in a manner similar to pain: it creates discomfort that the subject tries to reduce. Hence, the skewed messages conveyed by light and sound provoke an intense involvement on the part of the audience member who feels the need to reduce the dissonance the play generates.

Robert M. Post uses the notion of dissonance to analyze the discrepancies between the professed beliefs and the behaviors of major characters in Albee's early plays.[6] Post demonstrates that the behavior of George and Martha in Who's Afraid of Virginia Woolf? and that of Tobias and Agnes in A Delicate Balance reveal their need to reduce dissonance by making their actions consistent with their utterances. Tobias, for instance, is torn between his love for his friends and his desire for privacy. When Harry and Edna arrive at his door one night, shaken by their fear to sleep in their own house, Tobias offers them his bedroom. He has said he would help them if they ever needed his help. But when they decide to move in for an indefinite period of time, he resents their intrusion. Tobias is caught between his past promises and his present feelings.

Tobias's dilemma is not unique. As Post points out, the gap between a character's behavior and his or her speeches is one consequence of the "reality-illusion duality"[7] with which drama is preoccupied. But Post contends that Albee is unique in "attempting to create a cognitive dissonance in his audience."[8] Although those of us in the audience may know how it feels to agonize as Tobias does when he must decide whether or not to open his home to his friends, none of us need to make the choice at that moment. We may be acutely aware of how hypocritical Tobias's proclaimed love for Harry and Edna will be if he cannot offer them refuge from their fear, but no one invades our homes— nor are our words of love being tested. It is our privilege to observe Tobias, even sympathize with him, secure in the knowledge that no decision is expected of us. The audience of A

Delicate Balance does not experience cognitive dissonance first hand, as Post suggests; at best, the experience is vicarious. In other words, Albee has not revealed a discrepancy between the beliefs of each spectator and his or her behavior. The character's dissonance is dramatized, not ours. Traditionally in theatre, particularly in tragedy, the audience suffers vicariously with the hero; but our role remains empathetic and our participation in the drama strictly delimited. Part of what allows us to be more sympathetic toward characters on a stage than we usually are toward strangers on the street is our foreknowledge that no action is expected of us in the theatre, contrary to our fears outside.

Virginia Woolf and Delicate Balance, Post's arguments notwithstanding, are concerned solely with the dissonance experienced by the characters in the plays. In Albee's later plays Box and Quotations from Chairman Mao Tse-tung, however, he employs a fragmentary, non-narrative structure that violates preconceived notions of what a play should be and thereby induces his audience to experience cognitive dissonance for themselves. Box and Quotations are sufficiently dissonant that the audience must struggle to make sense of what they are seeing and hearing. Michael E. Rutenberg describes the spectator's experience as follows:

> instead of viewing a succession of events occurring in a cause-and-effect pattern, he is bombarded with simultaneous stimuli presented configurationally—the parts to be put together at another time.[9]

Rutenberg rightly suggests that the "polyphonic, non-narrative structure"[10] creates a kind of stream-of-consciousness that encourages us in the audience to associate freely the parts among ourselves, thereby moving the focus of the drama off the stage and into our heads.[11] It is audience dissonance, rather than character dissonance, that is being dramatized. The overriding dramatic action is not the characters' search for consonance, but the audience's struggle to reduce dissonance.

The fragmentary nature of both Box and Quotations, as well as the heightened involvement they demand of the audience, are consequences of the separation of sight and sound. Rutenberg discusses the polyphonic structure of the fragmented and intercut monologues that compose acoustic space but fails to note that visual and acoustic space are non-synchronous and that their arrangement, like that of the monologues, is contrapuntal. It is this larger, dissonant structure that involves the audience immediately, but it has not received the critical analysis it deserves.

A similar argument can be made of the scholarship on Pinter's *Landscape* and *Silence*. Peter Davison, for example, focuses on the "dislocation" caused by the expectations Pinter creates but does not fulfill in these two one-act plays.[12] Davison connects Pinter's use of pauses and silences to the music hall tradition of "silent puns," in which the performer pauses after a series of lines and allows the audience to extend and complete the thought before delivering an entirely unexpected line: "The resulting dislocation has . . . a comic effect."[13] Davison draws a parallel with Pinter's technique in *Landscape* and *Silence* where the effect is not comic, but dramatic: "There is a tension built up between the stage dialogue and the thoughts of each individual member of the audience," and this tension draws the audience into "active participation" in creating the meaning of the play.[14]

But Davison, like Post and Rutenberg, fails to see how the "dislocation" he has discovered is part of a larger scheme of dissonance in *Landscape* and *Silence*. This dislocation makes these two one-act plays a different sort of theatre than either the music hall or most of Pinter's other work.

Beckett's critics, on the other hand, acknowledge more frequently the audience's crucial role in his plays. Fletcher and Spurling, for example, argue that the action of *Play* draws the audience into "taking part";[15] and Karen Laughlin, in her extended discussion of the role of the spotlight in *Play*, concludes that it is the audience who must integrate the text and make sense of the play.[16] But how or why a spectator would take on such a role or what kind of theatre is being invented by playwrights who ask their audiences to integrate fragmentary dramatic pieces are questions left unanswered. The purpose of this study is to explore such questions, to follow the leads provided by existing scholarship, but to move the discussion beyond the stage into the minds of the audience.

The plays examined here violate traditional patterns of coherence, yet they are not incoherent. Their lack of coherence is only apparent because the usual means of providing unity, by creating harmony among the parts, has been abandoned in favor of a unity of effect. Their fragmentary structure is like a puzzle: the visual and verbal whole has been splintered in such a way that it requires intense spectator effort to reconstruct it. The conflicts these playwrights create between the visual and auditory media shift the center of dramatic action away from the usual conflict between characters and ideas. Here, audience members become protagonists in the central struggle taking place within our minds as we try to put the plays back together, i.e., create consonance out of dissonance.

"Consonance," "dissonance," and "harmony" are terms borrowed from music. Their application to drama indicates the similarity of the two performing arts. George Devine, in his program note to the British National Theatre production of *Play*, which he directed, compares the dramatic text to "a musical score wherein the 'notes,' the sights, the sounds, the pauses, have their own special inter-related rhythms, and out of their composition comes the dramatic impact."[17] But while composers have traditionally produced combinations of pleasing tones we call harmonies, contemporary composers deliberately create sharp discords.

Martin Esslin, in his influential study *The Theatre of the Absurd*, points out that in a musical context "absurd" means "out of harmony."[18] Esslin discusses Beckett, Albee, and Pinter, but he focuses on their earlier plays, works that precede the one-act plays examined here. Although these later pieces clearly show the influence of the Absurdist tradition, they do not entirely fit Esslin's definition. Dissonant theatre is a second-generation development from Absurdist drama, an extension of and deviation from the Absurd, achieved largely by means of a new technique: the deliberate disjunction of sight and sound. Esslin characterizes Absurd plays as "striving for an *integration* between the subject matter and the form";[19] the theatre of discord works toward *disintegration*. Absurdist theatre "communicate[s] a pattern of poetic images" intended "to make in the spectator's mind a total, complex impression";[20] dissonant plays communicate conflicting images. Where Absurd works create *pictures* of disintegration, dissonant works are *themselves disintegrating*. Where Absurdism *represents* chaos, the theatre of discord *reproduces* it. These plays extend the degree of audience involvement characteristic of Theatre of the Absurd by creating cognitive dissonance in the minds of the audience that requires us, if we are to come to terms with the work, to integrate the play's images ourselves. These one-act plays of Beckett, Albee, and Pinter, then, constitute a theatre of discord, in which the dramatic impact comes not from the integration of varied sounds in harmony but from the clashing of dissonant chords.

The theatre of discord restricts character activity almost exclusively to speech, thus heightening, by initially frustrating, the spectator's efforts to make the play meaningful. Plot—the arrangement of events in the lives of the characters—no longer unifies and orders the spectator's experience of the play; in fact, the narrative is fragmented to further generate dissonance. The disassociative structure is intended initially to disorient us and violate our conventional expectations; the eventual intention is to goad us to be more creative in our performance as co-producers of meaning.

2

The Battle of Lights and Voices:
Beckett's *Play* and *Breath*

Samuel Beckett's *Play* is a clear example of the separation of acoustic and visual space. A single spotlight controls speech. This reverses the usual relation of language and light on stage: typically, the lighting technician takes cues from the actors' speeches. In *Play*, however, light controls language. The actors speak only when illuminated; the spotlight moves from face to face, dictating the order and timing of the speeches. Beckett intends that speech be a response to light: "Speech is *provoked* by a spotlight projected on faces alone. . . . The *response to light* is not quite immediate. At every *solicitation* a pause of about one second before utterance is achieved."[1] The characters are nearly reduced to being mere instruments of sound. Both movement and facial expression are denied them. They are "held fast" in the mouths of "three identical grey urns. . . . They face un-deviatingly front throughout the play. Faces so lost to age and aspect as to seem almost part of urns. . . . Faces impassive throughout" (*Play*, 9). Even their vocal range is severely restricted: "Voices toneless except where an expression is indicated" (*Play*, 9). The actors are limited to monotone verbal responses to the spotlight.

However, their relation to the light is more complex than that of mere respondents. Although the three characters imprisoned in the urns never address each other and seem to be unaware of the others' presence, the movement of the spotlight from one face to another implies a complex relation among them. The stories the spotlight "solicits" are really one story, and a clichéd one at that: the eternal triangle of a man, his wife, and his lover, fraught with the usual pain, indignation, and lies. Each character tells a part of the story in his or her monologue, but the three monologues are intercut and woven together by the spotlight's movement from face to face. The characters' speeches are brief enough to sound like dialogue, one speech following another, but are actually a series of fragments from three continuous monologues. The characters do not appear to speak in any consistent pattern; the spotlight seems entirely capricious in its movements, as if it were, in Katherine Worth's words, "making the play . . . out of the individual narratives."[2]

Beckett once suggested that the text is divided into three parts: "Chorus," "Narration," and "Meditation."[3] Each part is separated from the following one by a brief blackout. A fourth part, the "Reprise," must be added, however, because the entire text is performed twice. At the end of the "Meditation," Beckett's directions say, "Repeat play exactly" (Play, 22).

The "Chorus" is a brief introductory passage in which the three urn characters speak simultaneously, muttering a collage of lines taken from the rest of the play. Like the first movement of a fugue, the "Chorus" hints of themes to come.

The "Narration" that follows reveals the man's relation to each of the women. Beckett uses the three viewpoints of his urn characters to create three different, although complementary, versions of the affair. The First Woman, the wife, relates the incidents of the triangular relationship from her discovery of her husband's affair to her confrontation with his mistress. The Second Woman completes the story by beginning with that confrontation and concluding with the Man's departure from her life. The Man's monologue covers the entire affair, from his wife's discovery of the adultery to his realization that "it was all too much" (Play, 9), implying that he then stopped seeing the Second Woman. This familiar plot is replete with the usual clichés: the detective hired by the suspecting wife, the husband's confession, the promises to go away together, and lines like "What he could have found in her when he had me" or "I could not go on living without her" (Play, 13, 14).

While the "Narration" reveals the characters' shared past, the final section, "Meditation," takes place in the present. The characters reflect on their present imprisonment in the urns and their isolation in a darkness broken only by the persistent spotlight compelling them to speak. Both the Man and the Second Woman prefer their current state to the affair they have just described; at least they feel this way initially. The Man begins the "Meditation" saying, "When first this change I actually thanked God. I thought, 'It is done . . .'" (*Play*, 15). A few lines later the Second Woman expresses the same preference: "I prefer this to . . . the other thing." Both compare "the other thing" with their present situation, what Beckett calls "their state of being endlessly suspended in limbo."[4] There is an implication that adultery led to their being in limbo, because each of the monologues in the "Narration" ends with an image of isolation, suggesting that their present condition is a continuation of the hell they created for themselves. Ironically, their life on earth, rather than their postmortem existence, is equated with hell. Although their preference for limbo over that previous hell seems to suggest that their lot is improving, the "Reprise" denies any such redemption. The wife's last speech before the blackout between "Narration" and "Meditation"—"I drove over to her place. It was all bolted and barred. All grey with frozen dew" (*Play*, 14)—conveys the isolation and imprisonment that prefigures her present confinement to an urn. Both she and the Second Woman are eventually abandoned by the Man, and their loneliness in life anticipates their solitary confinement in limbo. Their solitude, heightened by the disjunctive movements of the spotlight between their speeches, underlines the similarity between the two situations, their past and present suffering.

The spotlight, which serves as an unidentified "inquisitor" in the "Narration" (*Play*, 23), becomes the center of the urn characters' attention in the "Meditation." It is both the object to which the three faces articulate their meditations—they address it as "you"—and the subject of their meditations. The First Woman wants the spotlight to "get off" her, yet she worries that the light will "weary of playing with [her]." She regards the light as she might a disappointing lover. She both craves the darkness that will surround her when the light is gone and fears it: "Dying for dark—and the darker the worse. Strange" (*Play*, 21). She senses that her silent inquisitor wants her to tell more, to tell the truth that will placate the light and bring the darkness: "Is it that I do not tell the truth, is that it, that some day somehow I may tell the truth at last and then no more light at last, for the truth?" (*Play*, 16). Her response is ambivalent because the promise of silence and darkness brings with it the threat of utter solitude. On the one hand, the light is a clarifying conscience, or inner light, nagging the characters to persist in their meditations; on the other hand, it has become a surrogate partner, a replacement for the lost lover—or lovers, in the Man's case.

The end of the inquisition promises the same release from torment the characters expected at the end of their triangular affair, but which did not arrive then and will not arrive now. The "Reprise" dashes all hopes for an end to their suffering, implying an endless cycle of repetition; yet the characters persist. The wife imagines a time when it will be "all dark, all still, all over, wiped out" (Play, 9). Although the limbo she is in gives her "a certain amount of both," she is still not satisfied (Play, 21). The Second Woman voices her dissatisfaction at the outset of the "Meditation": "To say I am not disappointed, no, I am. I had anticipated something better. More restful" (Play, 15). It is the Man who most clearly articulates the common hopes of the urn characters. He assumed that "all the pain" would disappear "as if . . . never been" (Play, 10). In spite of the incessant light, he still imagines that the darkness and rest he desires "will come. Must come. There is no future in this" (Play, 16). Ironically, the implication of the exact repetition of the text of the "Reprise" is that this is his future.

However, the Man's hopes for an end to "all the pain" alternate with his fear of losing his sole companion, what he calls the "mere eye" of the spotlight (Play, 21). Without it, he is alone in the darkness, undefined and unknown. The light verifies his existence. Of paramount importance, then, is that he is being watched. "To be is to be perceived," Bishop Berkeley's famous dictum, is reversed in this case: I am perceived, therefore I am. The Man's last line in the "Meditation" asks the spotlight to confirm that it is indeed watching: "Am I as much as . . . being seen?" (Play, 22). It is the question a doubting theist asks of god. Of course, the god—here embodied in the light—cannot answer, except to turn the light on the suppliant's face again, leaving the Man uncertain whether he is being watched or whether he has been abandoned.

Although the light's solicitations discomfort the characters, they fear its "going out" because, alone except for its presence, their lives—or what remains of them, i.e., their verbal lives—are inextricably linked to its life: "When you go out—and I go out"

(*Play*, 16). They show no signs of being aware of each other, only of the light. It has replaced the lover or spouse in each of their lives—they can talk to it or be watched by it. They are prisoners of the whimsical light and of the urns much as they were prisoners of their lovers and spouses: behavior must be justified and explanations offered. In both the "Narration" and the "Meditation," each character yearns to be free of the "other," whether lover or light, but fears being alone. This internal conflict is most evident in the "Meditation," while the obvious external conflicts among the characters is shown in the "Narration."

But the more important conflict, that between the spotlight and the characters, is central to the three sections—"Chorus," "Narration," "Meditation"—as well as to the "Reprise." In fact, the verbatim repetition of *Play* makes it obvious that the central conflict is not among the urn characters but between the liberating potential of language and the arbitrary, inviolable authority of the light that locks the characters into the endless replay of the past. Although confession is typically a way to free ourselves from the past, the characters' confessions elicited by the light have no power of absolution. The women and man are doomed to retell, and relive in the retelling, their tormented past. The mechanical light frustrates any potentially liberating experience of verbalizing their pain. Language battles with light, and the outcome is dissonance between the verbal and visual media.

Play's title has been described as a "pun on adultery,"[5] perhaps because the "Narration" is little more than a recapitulation of the trio's playing around, a conventional triangular love plot, albeit dramatized in an unusual and often difficult manner. *Play* would be no more than that were it not for the central role of the spotlight. The conflicts in the "Narration" are remembered, not enacted. The "Narration" would be an entirely static reading of three separate monologues, without any of the conflicts between characters that move a play from beginning to end, were it not for the spotlight intercutting the three monologues and suggesting conflict by juxtaposing speeches. For example, it is never stated that the Man deceives both women—each woman wants to believe that he loves her only. Nor is his abandonment of them dramatized by a scene in which one of the women discovers his deceit. Yet his deception is clearly implied by the juxtaposition of the following speeches:

Second Woman. The only solution was to go away together. He swore we should as soon as he had put his affairs in order. In the meantime we were to carry on as before. By that he meant as best we could. [*Spot from W2 to W1.*]

First Woman. So he was mine again. All mine. I was happy again. I went about singing . . . (*Play,* 14)

The two events—the promise to "go away together" and the First Woman's happiness—do not occur at the same time. The wife (First Woman) gloats about having her husband back after the first confrontation between the two women, but the Man promises his mistress (Second Woman) a trip after the second confrontation. Beckett juxtaposes the two memories to heighten the sense of past conflict between the women and to reveal the Man's duplicity.

Despite its pivotal role in the "Narration," the spotlight remains unidentified, neither addressed nor referred to in that section. Its central role does become apparent in the "Meditation": it is the antagonist in the struggle between language and light. The division between acoustic and visual space is clearest in this section. As Katherine Worth notes, "Light is [Beckett's] chief tool for creating this sense of double space."[6] The characters, denied movement and facial expression, fill acoustic space with their words. The light, on the other hand, is in constant motion, but silent. Although the characters prefer silence and darkness, the spotlight provokes their speech by flooding their faces with light. This struggle between inquisitor and prisoners is never in doubt because they cannot refuse to speak when light strikes their faces.

The spotlight plays many roles and fills many functions for the characters, but in each its power is stymied. It is an inquisitor who can ask no questions, a confessor who offers no absolution, a god who commands no faith, a lover who provides no satisfaction. Yet the spotlight controls the characters. Although it can neither alter their situation nor permit their escape, the light can and does control their one activity, speech. It is a mechanical despot, both literally and figuratively, for its regime is purposeless, yet it gains nothing for its manipulation of the characters.

The tension generated between the tyranny of the light and the characters' desire to end their suffering is as static as that between the characters themselves. There is no hope for change, no chance that the tension will be resolved. Yet, despite the utter predictability of the situation, the polarization of the source of light and the source of language captivates an audience. Where the light moves, we look. Trapped in a dark auditorium, our responses (at least the physical responses necessary for sensory perception) are manipulated by the same light that controls the characters. "We are as much passive sufferers of the light as the heads are," John Pilling notes.[7] This, then, is the central analogy of Beckett's theatre, that the spectators are just as much prisoners as the characters. Unless we choose to leave the theatre, we spectators have no more choice in what we want to hear and see than the actors have in what they must perform. The script is our common prison. For a prescribed time, neither the audience nor the actors can alter the script. The analogous relationship between the actors on the stage and the audience in their seats suggests that the characters' situation, imprisoned in urns, is a metaphor for the audience's, imprisoned in a dark theatre. Both wait for a Godot-like character whose non-arrival is a certainty. Or, to borrow the metaphor from another Beckett play, audience and actors are conjoined to play out the final moves of an elaborate game, the outcome of which is known beforehand.

This analogous relationship between the audience and the urn characters manifests itself in several ways. Both want to know the purpose behind the light's chaotic movements, and both are dependent on its illumination: literally, because it is the only light used in the performance, and figuratively, because its inquisition promises metaphoric illumination.[8] Spectator and character share what Robert Wilcher calls "a single experience of deprivation and confinement."[9] Beckett has broken down "the distinctions between the objective 'stage picture' of deprivation, the deprivation imposed upon the actors, and the deprivation imposed upon the spectators,"[10] thereby realizing physically the analogy of audience and character/actor.

But another analogy is working here as well. When the Man asks, "Am I as much as . . . being seen?" (Play, 22), his question is directed at both audiences, the spotlight and the paying customers. For him, both are "mere eye[s]." The location of the spotlight in the theatre reinforces these similarities between light and spectator. Beckett's directions say, "The source of light . . . must not be situated outside the ideal space (stage) occupied by its victims. . . . The optimum position for the spot is at the centre of the footlights" (*Play*, 23). This makes the light visible to the audience, as if it were in the front row. If it were located in the usual position for a spotlight, above and behind the audience, the analogy would not be so striking. In the location Beckett cites as optimum, the light becomes, in Shoshana Avigal's words, a "stage-representative of the spectator's role."[11] Hugh Kenner calls the spot "a metaphor for *our* attention (relentless, all-consuming, whimsical)."[12]

Play illustrates one way inter-character conflict can be relocated in the minds of the spectators: using a spotlight that serves both as antagonist to the victimized characters and as a metaphorically victimized spectator. This dual role underscores the ambivalent role of the audience. At one and the same time we sympathize with the characters' suffering (sensing their dilemma is ours), while knowing we are the cause of that suffering, the very reason they persist. If the audience left or the light went out, their playing would end.

To achieve a balance in the audience's dual role, Beckett uses three techniques to counter the conventional, perhaps natural, impulse of the audience to sympathize with the characters: the metaphoric connection between the roles of the spotlight and the audience, the repetition of the entire play, and the rapid tempo of the performance. Both the visible presence of the light and the repetition of the text in the "Reprise" are theatrical devices that distance an audience from characters by making the audience aware of the performance as performance. A visible light source reminds us that we are in a theatre, that what we see is staged and lighted for our benefit. In a similar although more forceful manner, the repetition of the entire play frustrates the impulse to view the characters as real persons deserving sympathy. Hearing them describe their affair, isolation, and discomfort a second time, in exactly the same words, permits us to re-view the play as a whole. The second time through, however, we notice the artifice—the light and "Reprise" being the most startling examples because they are unusual—as well as the art.

But it is the rapid tempo of the performance that is likely to frustrate an audience the most. Beckett's directions for rapid speech make even more difficult the task of following the three

monologues and piecing together the story. It is what Wilcher
describes as "the toneless gabble of the voices and unpredictable
switching from one face and one version of the story to another"[13] that make it seem as though the audience must struggle
against the text and the performance. The quiet and "largely
unintelligible" voices the stage directions call for during the
chorus (Play, 9), as well as the rapid delivery of the entire text,
seem to imply that Beckett is intentionally obscuring his play;
however, he is directing our attention to the work's focus, "the
fundamental confrontation of perceiver and perceived."[14] Our
difficulty hearing the characters focuses our attention on what
we see; the physical setting, as metaphor for our role as spectators, is emphasized over the plot line of the triangular love
affair. The play is so abstracted that the characters are mere
pawns of the light, and their story is no more than a formula. The
dramatic tension assumed to exist between characters is dis-
placed by the tension between the acoustic clichés and the ar-
resting visuals.

The discordant juxtaposition of clichéd language and the original use of light creates cognitive dissonance for the audience.
What Andrew Kennedy calls the "indestructible" connection of
action and language[15] is, for the duration of the performance,
broken. The rupture of sight and sound draws Beckett's audience
into what Worth calls "a disturbing and releasing experience of
inwardness and heightened perception."[16] The "heightened perception" is a consequence of the audience's need to reduce dissonance, while the "inwardness" of the experience comes from the
discovery of the double analogy of audience:actor and au-
dience:light. Wherever we look we see ourselves.

> And once this process has been set in motion, the action on stage
> reflecting the experience it gives rise to in the audience, the au-
> dience's experience reflecting back on the action on stage, the almost
> impossible is achieved: the audience, instead of simply witnessing
> and reacting to patterns of sight and sound placed at some remove, is
> drawn into them."[17]

Stage action, then, reflects audience experience; and Beckett's
set serves as an analogue for the human mind. Both the spotlight,
in its efforts to elicit and order the characters' stories, and the
audience, similarly engaged, are attempting to create meaning,

while the characters are trying to *convey* meaning. This implies that the physical separation of sight (the light) and sound (the actors) within view of the audience is analogous to the separation of audience and artist. Just as the urn characters want to communicate their meaning—story, feelings—to their audience, the light, the playwright also wishes to express himself to his audience. The difference lies in the restrictions Beckett places upon his actors; unlike the playwright they are limited almost entirely to verbal expression. Beckett, however, dramatizes his meaning both visually and acoustically. The startling handicaps he imposes on actors suggest metaphorically both the difficulties the artist faces and the real barriers his audiences must overcome. The intellectual and emotional "distance" an audience must travel to arrive at the artist's vantage point and to see the work through the creator's eyes is symbolized by the distance between the light and urns. The fragmentation of monologues and the repetition of the text without resolution invites the audience to become co-creators of the work's meanings. We can "play" too—inventing analogies, metaphors, and meanings to explain our experience—while being directed by the light. The faces trapped in the urns serve as visual metaphors for our minds trapped by conventions, expectations, and innate limitations.

The arrested action of *Play* is a metaphor for the audience's inability to resolve their dilemma.[18] The characters are certainly powerless to change their situation, but the traditionally passive spectators are also impotent to alter the circumstances of their experience. When the Man calls the spotlight a "mere eye" with "no mind" (*Play*, 21), he is implicating the spectator as well. Beckett seems to be goading his audience to transcend their passivity—which the characters cannot do—and engage themselves more in *Play*. This invitation is limited primarily to intellectual involvement—it does not include physically joining the cast (as Environmental Theatre did in the 1960s)—and is most evident in the direction to replay the entire text. As we in the audience grow more conscious of our part and of the analogous relation of the light's activity to our own attempts at establishing the play's meaning, we are able to see the play anew. For the actors, the "Reprise" is simply static repetition. For the audience, however, *Play* is a new work the second time around, to paraphrase Kenner,[19] filled with unresolved conflicts and dissonances. If, the first time through *Play*, we focus on the relations among characters, specifically the adultery, upon a second viewing we are more likely to focus on the relation between the characters and the spotlight. After the story of the affair is told, there is no more to be revealed, but the conflict between light and speech is continually dramatized. This central conflict between the tyranny of light and the suffering of the urn faces cannot be observed at a safe distance; it plays itself out in our heads. We are imprisoned in the same darkness and obedient to the same moving light as the characters, but we also imprison them. The monologues are spoken for us, as much as for the light. As audience we are polarized between our sympathy for the characters and the realization, driven home so forcefully by the analogy of the roles of spotlight and audience, that we are the cause of the characters' suffering. Both the First Woman and the Man directly implicate their audiences, spotlight and crowd, in their suffering. In one of the few lines for which Beckett indicates an exception to the toneless voices his directions call for, the First Woman tells the light to "Get off me! *(Vehement.)* Get off me!" (*Play*, 16). Later the Man describes both the light and the audience as an eye "opening and shutting on me" (*Play*, 21). It is the cruelty of voyeurism from the audience and the light that the characters must endure. Their only hope for escape lies in the fading of the light, which will bring silence and peace—and perhaps death. The characters wait in their urns for the light and spectators to "weary of playing" with them (*Play*, 21). In the performances he directed in London and Paris in 1964, Beckett had the light fade during the "Reprise" to suggest the wearying of light, character, and audience.[20]

The final blackout brings to a close what Kennedy calls "a succession of still points."[21] Actor movement in *Play* is entirely verbal, a seemingly endless string of words that creates the illusion of motion and direction but is static. *Play*, then, is built upon a "paradox of dramatic stasis"[22]—Beckett dramatizes inactivity. Character activity is diminished, and audience activity is heightened. Stasis on stage is dramatized off stage as the static is made dramatic.

Even the promise of an ending, which would imply some change in the "static quo," is denied. *Play* ends by beginning for a third time. After the "Reprise," the "Chorus" is repeated, and the opening line of the "Narration" is spoken before the curtain falls. This false start suggests that dropping the curtain at this point is merely a convenience for the audience, permitting them to leave the theatre, and that in fact *Play* does not end. Beckett's drama is characterized by this non-ending ending. In *Godot*, Vladimir and Estragon do not leave; they are still waiting when the curtain falls. Nor does Clov exit at the end of *Endgame*; action is stalemated. This use of an ending that implies another beginning is also seen in *Breath*, a later and much briefer piece than *Play*.

The human condition in *Breath*, as in *Play*, is imprisonment in a collapsing, decaying world. The stage is covered with scattered rubbish that includes no verticals, as Beckett explains in the stage directions.[23] Nothing is left standing; everything is fallen, collapsed, decayed. No life can be seen, but life is there. After five seconds of silence, dominated by a dim light, we hear a "faint brief cry and immediately inspiration" as someone, somewhere, takes a breath. Beckett carefully calls this inhaling "inspiration" (literally, a "breathing in") to clarify the analogy of life and art as similar creative processes. Inspiration lasts ten seconds during which the lighting on stage increases. This implies that as the unseen someone breathes and lives, the world grows brighter. Things are illuminated; light becomes a metaphor for both understanding (enlightenment) and hope (a brightened outlook).

The ten-second inspiration is followed by a five-second silence and then a ten-second expiration with accompanying decreased light and a cry as before. A five-second silence follows, the stage is lit dimly as it was at the opening, and then the curtain falls. The extreme brevity of *Breath*, thirty-five seconds, suggests the brevity of human life. Beckett's emphasis is on human suffering: we come into this garbage-heap world with a cry and exit moments later with another. As Hersch Zeifman points out, *Breath* is a "gloss for *Waiting for Godot*, a striking dramatization of Pozzo's chilling metaphor: 'They give birth astride of a grave, the light gleams an instant, then it's night once more.' "[24]

Partly because of its brevity, *Breath* is often considered Beckett's bleakest drama. A. Alvarez originally described it as "literally, that last gasp."[25] Alvarez expected no more plays from Beckett: "It is difficult to see where he can go on to." After the appearance of *Not I*, the play that followed *Breath* and preceded a series of critically noteworthy short pieces, Alvarez admitted his short-sightedness.[26] But the reductive interpretation of Breath as a last gasp, a dead end for the playwright, persists. The brevity and starkness of the piece have been the focus of attention and are the reason for this dismal conclusion. But the action, although strictly limited, has been overlooked.

The play is composed simply of the two theatrical elements, light and sound, presented to the audience without the usual set and speeches. Beckett does this to emphasize the subtle conflict between what we see and what we hear. Clearly the setting is one of his bleakest; but he has used barren, depressing, hellish, prison-like settings before in his often hopeful plays. In Happy Days, for instance, Winnie, although buried alive before the audience, remains cheerful, even hopeful about life. In Godot, despite the futility of their existence, Vladimir and Estragon become symbols of human compassion. Even the impassive urn faces of Play are humanized by their suffering. In Breath, therefore, the extremely pessimistic statement about the human condition implied by a stage covered with rubbish should not be misconstrued as the playwright's message. Although Beckett's settings are often bleak, his language often suggests optimism.

The depressing judgment of the modern world with its refuse and decay implicit in Breath's setting is contrasted by the hopeful brightening light as the breath is taken. Whereas in Play the spotlight controls the characters and imposes its mechanical rhythm on their utterances, the human sounds in Breath, crying and breathing, provide the rhythm for the light. Breath visually appears less human because no characters appear, but it is more human because it is informed by the rhythms of life and death. When someone breathes, light increases. The light is the literal source of illumination and brightening, the metaphoric source of both understanding (illuminating the darkness of ignorance) and hope (brightening the prospects for the future). It is humanized by its association with human sounds, especially the breath, which is a metaphor for creative inspiration. It is our imaginative power, then, that determines how we see the world—our ability to use inspiration to illuminate our setting. Every life becomes a creative as well as a procreative act, as Beckett playfully puns on the analogy inherent in the word "inspiration."

Beckett sees hope in the bleak setting and in the brevity of human lives because human sound in Breath—a proto-language of scream and sigh—controls the mechanical light, the opposite of what happens in Play. We hear the cry, then "immediately inspiration and slow increase of light together," then expiration, decrease of light, and the same cry. The two cries are an identical instant of recorded birth. The initial sound of human life, the cry at birth, initiates the dramatic action. That action, which consists only in the brightening and dimming of light, is controlled by the human rhythm of breathing. The inspiration part of a breath increases light and, by extension, hope and understanding. The expiration, the movement toward death, signals the decrease in light. Beckett does not deny the brevity of human life, nor the difficulty of understanding, nor the pain suffered—he isolates those qualities of existence and heightens them, compelling us to recognize our nature. But Beckett's emphasis on the brevity and pain of life is not reason enough to conclude that Breath implies all is futile. Two things invalidate such an interpretation. (1) Human life is not ruled by an arbitrary force, as in Play, nor defeated by the bleakness of the setting; rather, humans impose their rhythms upon the world. (2) Because the birth cry that initiates the action also concludes it, birth and death are linked in a cycle, suggesting an unending series of births and deaths. The last scream is not just a scream of death marking the end of the ten-second exhalation; it is also the scream of new birth, ushering in another moment, however brief, of inspiration. A balance is struck. As Yasanuri Takahashi describes it, "Death will not prevail so easily, and life will consist not in pure silence, but in a never-to-be-resolved tension between scream and silence, between death-principle and life-principle."[27]

Both Breath and Play dramatize this unresolved tension between silence and scream, darkness and light, death and life, through the separation and opposition of acoustic and visual space. As the titles suggest, these works, although brief and limited in action, are concerned with fundamental human activities. To avoid the multifarious clichés and truisms customarily associated with such subjects as the dichotomy of life and death, Beckett jars his audience with the clash of sight and sound, which he describes as "the battle, lights and voices."[28] The resultant pressure of dissonance forges a new spectator, one able to see light in the darkness of Beckett's plays.

3

The Chinese Box:
Albee's *Box* and *Quotations from Chairman Mao Tse-tung*

In *Play*, light controls language; in *Breath*, sound (breathing) determines the level of light. In Edward Albee's twin plays, *Box* and *Quotations from Chairman Mao Tse-Tung*, however, the relationship between the visual and the verbal is more complex and ambiguous. First, these two plays actually constitute a single work, because Albee intended them to be performed "enmeshed," i.e., one play inside the other. As he explains in the preface, "While it is true that these two short plays . . . are separate works . . . I feel that they are more effective performed enmeshed."[1] Albee has created a series of Chinese boxes: first, the shorter play, *Box*, is performed, then *Quotations*, and finally a brief "Reprise" of *Box*. This structure led Michael Rutenberg to call the entire performance piece "*Box-Mao-Box*."[2] The set further suggests Chinese boxes: the deck of an ocean liner that is the setting for *Quotations* is contained within the "outline of a large cube" (*Box* and *Quotations*, 3), the setting for *Box*. Chairman Mao's play is boxed in both visually and acoustically, surrounded by the cube physically and the text of *Box* verbally. The word "box" appropriately begins and ends the performance; it is the container its name implies. As Ruby Cohn says, the box "does what it means."[3]

The box is a common Albee symbol. Grandma is buried in one filled with sand in *The Sandbox* and packs her life away in little ones in *The American Dream*; the dying man in *All Over* is soon to be boxed in a coffin; and Tiny Alice lives in a very curious set of Chinese boxes.[4] In each case, the box is a metaphor for the human environment, what Anthony Hopkins calls "the life

34

space" of each being and of all humankind.[5] All dramatic settings function this way to some degree, of course. In each of the plays above, however, with the exception of Tiny Alice perhaps, the box is a coffin—either a literal or symbolic one—the repository for a life that is "all over." Although Box and Quotations are as intricately structured as Chinese boxes, the hollow cube that fills the stage is ultimately another of Albee's symbolic coffins containing the empty lives of his characters. Acoustic space is filled with the noisy activity of fragmented and intercut monologues, much as in Play, but here the juxtaposition of verbal clamor against the unchanging visual symbol of the box reverberates the emptiness of the words. The box is silent and motionless, yet it holds all the conflict, turmoil, and movement of the characters. This opposition of visual stasis and acoustic frenzy is focused in the relationship between the word "box" and the object it names. The word is enriched by performance, its associations multiplied and altered from the opening syllable of the play—a matter-of-fact announcement, "Box"—to the final sad supplication, "Box" (Box and Quotations, 3, 74). The box, container of all we see and metaphor for all we hear, is unaltered. The lighting that illuminates it also does not change (Box and Quotations, 3). The static object contradicts the fluid word.

Box, comprised of a single monologue, is a perfect example of what Kennedy calls the "paradox of dramatic stasis."[6] There is no plot to chart the play's movement from beginning to end, no readily discerned and physically manifested conflict, no rising action, no crisis, no characters—nothing ordinarily called dramatic. The play is reduced to a space and a voice—a cube on a stage and a Voice speaking to the audience, not from the stage, but "from the back or the sides of the theater" so that it seems "to be coming from nearby the spectator" (Box and Quotations, 3). The location of Voice at the rear or sides of the theatre suggests that the audience, like the characters, are contained in Chinese boxes. The box on stage suggests the box of the stage (delineated by the proscenium arch and the stage floor), which in turn suggests the box of the theatre building itself.[7]

The nameless, bodiless Voice is that of a middle-aged Midwestern farm woman who speaks for approximately ten minutes[8] about "arts which have gone down to craft and which are going further" (Box and Quotations, 4). She mentions carpentry, music, and breadmaking as examples, concluding that "when art hurts . . . that is what to remember." The intimacy of Voice, as if she were standing beside us, suggests that we are being spoken for as much as to. When she speaks of declined art, she reminds us of the persistent rumors of the death of the theatre. Voice implies that this artistic decline is a consequence of a more general decline of Western civilization.

Voice's monologue is filled with images of loss: spilt milk, music that makes us cry, the mournful sounds of bell buoys and sea gulls, "seven hundred million babies dead," and art that "tells us what we cannot have" (Box and Quotations, 4–7). The orderliness of art is in such contrast to the waste and ruin around her—especially the spilt milk and dead babies—that it causes her pain: "when art hurts . . . when the beauty of it reminds us of loss" (Box and Quotations, 7). Art's orderliness then, reminds us how far civilization has declined; the box/coffin, a visual symbol of both art and its decline, hints of the empty future for civilization and its arts.

The "dramatic stasis" of Box, its lack of characters or conflict on stage, conveys to the audience the feelings of loss that Voice describes. Albee's form fits his subject perfectly. Anne Paolucci describes Box as having "no dramatic situation or setting . . . no progression; rather . . . repetitions of an eternal present."[9] Despite the severe limitations Albee has placed on dramatic action, Box is not entirely static. The conflict has been removed from the stage and transplanted to the minds of the audience.[10] To achieve this, Albee specifies that the Voice must seem to be speaking from very near us, the audience, almost as if we are hearing an interior monologue of our own. This effect is achieved because Voice's monologue resembles the stream-of-consciousness narration associated with interior monologue. This technique, coupled with the intimacy of Voice and the deprivation of visual space, allows us to feel the pain Voice describes as if it were our own—which in a sense it is.

Voice's monologue introduces the themes that are expanded in Quotations. Ronald Hayman defines the subject the two plays share as "the movement of our civilization towards holocaust."[11] The spectre of the box is a persistent reminder of the imminence and inevitability of death, both of civilization and the individual. The cube's empty presence bankrupts any attempts to ascribe meaning or significance to life. The drama that shapes *Box* and *Quotations* and qualifies them as theatre despite their seemingly undramatic form is the tension between the ineluctable stasis of personal or cultural morality and the persistent human struggle to create meaningful lives in spite of death. This conflict is implicit in the contrast between the static box and the protean language of the characters struggling to order their lives and their worlds. The only space in which the static visual and dynamic verbal can collide is in the mind of the spectator. As in *Play* and *Breath*, the audience is thrust into the center of the drama by the dissonance of the two media, sight and sound. That dissonance must be resolved if the audience is to comprehend, rationally or intuitively, Albee's play. To reduce the dissonance, each spectator must reenact the Voice's struggle to find order; consequently, each experiences the same sense of loss.

Voice's monologue culminates in her final image of a black net of birds skimming the ocean. Earlier she had been heartened by the orderly flight of the birds, but now she is saddened by their net-like appearance, which suggests a trap or perhaps death. With "great sadness" she sees a lone bird "moving beneath . . . in the opposite way" (*Box and Quotations*, 10). Perhaps she sees herself as the bird flying away from the net and shares its loneliness; or perhaps she fears the net is a trap and that this solo bird is also boxed in. This elusive image captures her ambiguous attitude toward order—the beauty she longs for, the death she fears. Her final lines, spoken sadly and supplicatingly, are a direct request to the audience for milk, presumably to replace the spilt milk she referred to earlier that might have nourished the starving children whose deaths she lamented (*Box and Quotations*, 6). After a silence she utters her final word, "Box," and apparently resigns herself to the fact that the audience cannot respond to her supplications, that they are as boxed in—by convention and role—as she.

During *Quotations from Chairman Mao Tse-tung*, fragments of Voice's monologue briefly interrupt the other speakers, and at the end of *Quotations* there is a reprise of *Box* that repeats central images of Voice's monologue. Because *Quotations* is not only significantly longer but more complex than *Box*, the tension between static visual space and dynamic acoustic space is often obscured. The length and variety of the verbal text threatens to

overwhelm the starkness and simplicity of the set; but the startling presence of the box in the midst of a play that takes place on
an ocean liner, as *Quotations* does, is an insistent reminder of the
disjunction of sight and sound.

   Quotations' setting is suggested by a railing and a pair of deck
chairs that appear "within the outlines of the cube during the
brief blackout" between *Box* and *Quotations* (*Box* and *Quotations*,12, 17). The cruise is a pretext for assembling four very
different characters in a single space: Chairman Mao, an Old
Woman, a silent Minister, and the Long-Winded Lady. The cruise
also serves as a metaphor for the characters' journeys through life
as well as a civilization's passage through history.

   Albee's stage directions carefully circumscribe the space
within which each character may move. Chairman Mao is to
"keep his place by the railing" as he speaks to the audience. The
Old Woman is to "stay in one place, up on something" as she
recites her poem to the audience. The Minister, who is silent
throughout the play, "stays in his deck chair" trying to listen
attentively to the Long-Winded Lady, but occasionally dozing off.
The Lady stays "pretty much to her deck chair" as she speaks to
the Minister (*Box* and *Quotations*, 13–15).

   Albee isolates his characters verbally as well as physically, and
he accomplishes this by using separate monologues: Mao's political speeches, the Old Woman's recitation of a narrative poem, the
Long-Winded Lady's narrative, and snatches from Voice's previous monologue. There is no dialogue. Both the verbal and
visual space occupied by each character is discrete. In the production Albee directed himself, however, he relaxed his restrictions on actor movement, permitting Chairman Mao to move
more freely about the stage. Perhaps the exigencies faced by a
company touring the States necessitated such compromises; or,
more likely, Albee discovered that the stasis he was trying to
create was alienating audiences. Although Mao is permitted
greater mobility, the chief characteristic *Quotations* shares with
Box remains its static quality. Physically, very little happens.
There is no motion of set, backdrop, or lighting to suggest the
movement of an ocean liner. Although Mao paces slowly and
rhythmically about the stage, occasionally sitting on the edge of
the stage and addressing the front row of the audience, he spends
most of his time standing still. The sporadic sudden movements

of the Long-Winded Lady—rising or sitting, turning toward or away from the Minister—never take her more than a few steps from her deck chair. Both the Minister and the Old Woman remain seated throughout the play, he on his deck chair and she on an old trunk. The cube itself, which dominates the stage, never moves. Its inertia weighs upon the limited motions of the characters; they cannot escape it. The entire effect creates, in Rutenberg's words, "a stillness . . . tightly congruent to the play's theme."[12]

The artifice of Quotations, its obvious theatricality, is also conveyed visually. The set is abstract: chairs and a railing suggest the deck of a ship, and the transparent cube is suspended above. In addition, Mao is a distinctive character both in his gestures and costume. In the production Albee directed, the actor's hand motions and rhythmic pacing were carefully choreographed, and he used two identical masks, caricatures of the former Chinese leader. The actor carried the first mask on a stick in front of his face. When he lowered this mask before his opening speech, the second mask was revealed, which covered his entire face except for his jaw (enabling him to speak without interference). During the pauses between his early speeches, he hid coyly behind the stick-mask. The Chairman's masks, like the Chinese boxes, are a series of containers, each of which opens to reveal yet another container. These devices suggest that Albee's enmeshed performance of Box and Quotations works analogically, setting up a series of correspondences that transfer symbolic meaning from one layer, or container, to the next, creating what Foster Hirsch calls "cosmic reverberations."[13]

The separate monologues and the discrete physical space between each character, coupled with the box on stage, suggest an invisible box isolating each of the characters, much as the urns separate the characters in Play. Like Beckett's characters, Albee's seem suspended in some ambiguous space between the lives they recall and the deaths they face. They are on a ship that is making a symbolic journey toward death.[14] Although Albee's characters exhibit much verbal liveliness, their extreme isolation implies that they are already trapped in their individual coffins.

Albee uses a technique similar to Beckett's in Play to fragment and intercut the monologues in Quotations, with one monologue seeming to interrupt another. The result often sounds like dialogue. For example, one of Voice's lines seems to be a response to Mao's previous speech rather than an echoing of her earlier monologue:

> Chairman Mao.   All reactionaries are paper tigers. In appearance, the reactionaries are terrifying, but in reality they are not so powerful. From a long-term point of view, it is not the reactionaries but the people who are really powerful.
> Voice, From Box.   Apathy, I think. (Box and Quotations, 33).

Voice seems to be correcting Mao's estimation of the political power of the masses. The juxtaposition of the two speeches undercuts Mao's political theory. In an earlier, similarly ironic juxtaposition, the Long-Winded Lady discovers the right word to describe the sound one makes falling into water:

> Plut! Yes!
> Chairman Mao.   . . . The communist ideological and social system alone is full of youth and vitality, sweeping the world with the momentum of an avalanche and the force of a thunderbolt.
> Long-Winded Lady.   Exactly: plut! (Box and Quotations, 20)

The avalanche and thunderbolt of communism are reduced to "plut."

Juxtaposed but unrelated monologues are one source of the cognitive dissonance Albee creates for his audience. The juxtapositioning of the two speeches creates an associative rather than narrative, or causal, structure that is unified by theme but not by plot. Although Albee's monologues, unlike Beckett's, are not connected by a common story, the four monologues voice the same themes and are counterpointed in what Albee calls an "experiment" with "musical structure" (Box and Quotations, 15). More specifically, Albee's musical model is a partita.[15] Themes are stated in the initial section (Box), developed and interwoven in the body of the composition (Quotations), and restated in the coda (reprise).

Except for the silent Minister, the characters in Quotations, all of whom are old and "winding down" their lives,[16] develop the themes of decline and death that Voice's imagery evoke. They each suffer from alienation: the Old Woman and Long-Winded Lady are rejected by their families, and Mao experiences the

global alienation of East and West. Consequently, they are searching for order to provide coherence and to reduce their sense of
loss. As Anne Paolucci points out, "Order is the absolute for
which the characters search vainly."[17]

Albee's musical structure, with its counterpointed themes and
juxtaposed speeches, creates complex analogues[18] that become a
new source for harmony within the work if we abandon our
expectation that a play will be unified by plot and action. Albee
warns his audience that the plays "demand . . . quite close attention" and a willingness to experience them on their own terms
"without a weighing of their methods against more familiar
ones" (Box and Quotations, ix, xi). The analogic structure com-
pels the audience to seek meaning in the thematic and imagistic
relationships among monologues and between visual and verbal
metaphors. C. W. E. Bigsby describes the process this way:

> The play's method forces the audience into an attempt to recon-
> struct . . . meaning, not by reassembling the shattered monologues
> but by relating them to each other in such a way as to become aware
> of the tenuous but real connections.[19]

The characters are united by the thematic content of their
speeches; the subject of their individual monologues as well as
their personal manner of presentation express their essential
isolation.

Chairman Mao's speech is as carefully stylized as his gestures
and masks. Mao "is not given to histrionics. His tone is always
reasonable" (Box and Quotations, 13) and his speeches always
delivered smoothly. There is no struggling for words, no unfilled
pauses or stutterings, no hesitations—none of the usual lapses
that characterize impromptu speech—because his is a prepared
text. All of Mao's speeches are taken verbatim from the famous
Red Book, Quotations from Chairman Mao Tse-tung.

During Quotations, Mao delivers what is, in effect, a political
lecture, composed of the speeches and writings in the Red Book.
Albee's notes indicate that he speaks "rather like a teacher" (Box
and Quotations, 13). Metaphor and allegory adorn his political
dichotomy of good guys, the Chinese masses, and bad guys,
principally American imperialists. He appeals to China's
glorious past while expressing unqualified optimism about the

power and goodness of the Chinese people. Ironically, he addresses this to an American audience. Mao's tone shifts during the play from the hopeful naïveté of his early statements about the coming revolution—"sooner or later revolution will take place and will inevitably triumph" (Box and Quotations, 35)—to a final bitterness in his attacks on "U.S. aggressors and . . . running dogs. . . . Monsters . . . [who] shall be destroyed" (Box and Quotations, 69). His extreme rhetoric is incongruous, delivered calmly as Albee indicates. Although his is a voice of promise in the beginning, Albee's arrangement of Mao's speeches reveals the bloody cost of those promises by the play's end. His claims that China is "firmly for peace and against war" (Box and Quotations, 49) are reversed by the later assertion that war is inevitable because "only with guns can the whole world be transformed" (Box and Quotations, 58). By arranging the contradictions in Mao's politics so that they are revealed to the audience a bit at a time and by undercutting the Chairman's message by ironically juxtaposing the other monologues, Albee distances Mao from his audience.

The Old Woman's mechanical recital of Will Carleton's poem "Over the Hill to the Poorhouse" similarly distances her despite her direct address to the audience (Box and Quotations, 14). The poem shows the same obvious artifice as Mao's political rhetoric, and the Old Woman's sing-song recitation further emphasizes the clichéd treatment Carleton accords the subject of the abuse of old people. In one doggerel verse after another, the self-pitying persona visits her children, each of whom rejects her, until her son commits her to the poor house.

> So they have shirked and slighted me,
>   an' shifted me about—
> So they have wellnigh soured me, an'
>   wore my old heart out;
> But still I've borne up pretty well,
>   an wasn't much put down,
> Till Charley went to the poor-master,
>   an' put me on the town.
>
> (Box and Quotations, 65–66)

The Old Woman is another of Albee's disenfranchised grandmothers, neither as articulate nor as endearing as Grandma in

The Sandbox and *The American Dream*, yet still capable of arousing our sympathies for her plight at the hands of the younger generation. Like the Chairman, the Old Woman is quoting a text, not her own but one on a subject "dear to her heart" (*Box and Quotations,* 14). During Albee's production, the Old Woman made it clear she was reciting a poem by reading the first few lines from a book. Her delivery was so sincere, as if she were the poem's persona, that at times she overcame the intrusive rhythm and rhyme scheme of Carleton's verse. As he does with Chairman Mao, Albee engages our sympathies with his characters' pleasing delivery style while alienating us with their texts. We are not permitted to disregard either the Old Woman or Mao as mere props. Both speak to the audience, demanding our attention with nearly continuous eye contact. Although both are types, incarnations of old age and socialist revolution, they not only provide the background against which we view the play's central character, the Long-Winded Lady, but they also represent the dissonant chords she struggles to resolve.

This "very average and upper middle class" sixty-year-old woman (*Box and Quotations,* 13), the Long-Winded Lady, delivers the only original and spontaneous monologue in *Quotations.* Her speeches are the rambling conversation of an articulate and loquacious middle-aged lady. She demonstrates Albee's talent for capturing the false starts, pauses, and repetitions of someone struggling to find the right words to explain experiences she has not yet fully assimilated. She ostensibly addresses her monologue to the silent Minister; but, as Albee notes, "more often she is speaking both for his benefit and her own" (*Box and Quotations,* 14). She is, therefore, distinguished from Mao and the Old Woman because she neither delivers a "canned" text nor addresses the audience. On the other hand, her monologue is linked thematically to theirs. The three stories she tells—her fall from the deck of an ocean liner on a previous voyage, her husband's messy death, and the offensive behavior of her daughter[20]—echo the same themes of loss and death found in the other monologues. Her convoluted monologue doubles back on itself time and again, jumping from one story to another as she is reminded of them, and she repeats the same information with slight variations as she tries to make sense of the central experiences of her recent life. She begins with her inexplicable fall from the deck of an ocean liner, similar to the one she is on now, into the water below.

> Well, I daresay it's hard to comprehend . . . I mean: I . . . at this remove . . . I find it hard to, well, not comprehend, but believe, or accept, if you will. So long ago! So much since. But there it was: Splash! (Box and Quotations, 18).[21]

After deciding "splash" does not capture the sound of her fall—eventually settling for "plut" (Box and Quotations, 20)—she considers how uncommon falling from an ocean liner really is and is suddenly reminded of "the time the taxi went berserk and killed those people!" (Box and Quotations, 25).

Ironically, the taxi memory is juxtaposed against Mao's attack on U.S. imperialism "riding roughshod everywhere" (Box and Quotations, 25). The collision of Mao's phrase and the Long-Winded Lady's taxi-on-the-loose monologue undercuts the seriousness of Mao's image by comparing imperialism to a car accident. Albee simultaneously connects the two speeches thematically by drawing attention to the catastrophes each speaker is explaining: the political catastrophe Mao aims to rectify through revolution and the personal catastrophe the Lady labors to comprehend. For the Lady, however, the taxi incident, like her fall from the ship deck, interests her primarily because it created cognitive dissonance. She walked out of a bakery into the middle of an accident, but the scene was so incongruous she did not realize what was happening at first. She describes her mental double-take:

> The bag of crullers, and a smile on my face for everyone liked them so, and there it was! Careen . . . and dying . . . and all that glass. And I remember thinking: it's a movie! . . . Oh, it was real enough, but it took me time to know it. The mind does that. (Box and Quotations, 26–27)

What the mind does, she says, is resolve the dissonant experience, even if the solution is wrong:

> One doesn't come out like that to carnage! Dead people and the wounded; glass all over and . . . confusion. One . . . concludes things—and if those things and what is really there don't . . . are not

the *same* . . . well! . . . it would usually be better if it were so. The mind does that: it helps. (*Box and Quotations*, 27)

Her memory of the taxi is linked with that of falling from the ship because both were so unusual and unexpected that she is unable to resolve the dissonance and make the incidents consonant with past experience. Her confusion during the taxi incident resolved a few moments after her initial shock, and she realized she was not witnessing a movie but an accident. Her fall, however, still puzzles her, even on this later voyage. She recalls the incident and rationalizes the story to the Minister to exorcise it.

The Lady's entire monologue is a search for consonance in her disparate experiences—her husband's death, the runaway taxi, and her rebellious daughter. Her efforts to impose an order on these disorderly memories recall Voice's yearning for order and make the Long-Winded Lady's fall a central image, the informing verbal metaphor, of *Quotations*. "The fall," Hirsch says, "becomes as suggestive and flexible an image as the primordial box that frames the two interrelated plays."[22]

Her fall represents both a literal and symbolic loss of innocence—not the moral innocence Adam and Eve lost, but a loss of faith in the stability and reliability of the physical universe. She discovers that even apparently solid, dependable structures such as deck railings can let one down:

> What can we say of an aging lady walks bright as you please from her rug and her Trollope or her James or sometimes her Hardy right up to the thing . . . the railing; walks right up, puts her fingers, rings and all, right on the varnished wood, sniffs . . . that air!, feels the railing, hard as wood, knows it's there—it *is* there—and suddenly, as sudden and sure as what you've always known and never quite admitted to yourself, it is *not* there; there is no railing, no wood, no metal, no buoy-life-thing . . . nothing! (*Box and Quotations*, 61)

The orderly, comprehensible worlds of Trollope, James, and Hardy have not prepared her for vanishing railings. Her discovery that external reality is occasionally unpredictable reveals something about herself, "what you've always known and never quite admitted to yourself"—a frank recognition of the irrational mystery at the core of experience and being. Her initial wonder at the fall changes to resignation when she realizes that the mind cannot always be relied on to explain experience:

One is suddenly leaning on one's imagination—which is poor support, let me tell you . . . at least in *my* case—leaning on that, which doesn't last for long, and over one goes! (*Box and Quotations*, 61)

Albee's fragmented text leaves us leaning on our imaginations as well, but they are poor support if we expect a traditionally ordered play.

The Lady is bewildered and pained by her fall. It reminds her of her husband's slow, painful death because neither her fall nor his death is fitting. She remembers him as "neat; accurate; precise. In everything. . . . Except dying, Except that . . . dreadful death" (*Box and Quotations*, 36). She tells the Minister that "the one thing you do *not* do is fall off the ship" (*Box and Quotations*, 59). Such behavior, like her husband's death, violates an implicit order she expects to find in life. She cannot believe that falling "by indirection" as she puts it, happens very often (*Box and Quotations*, 37). Because she expects to find direction, purpose, and order in life, she is shocked when her neat and precise husband dies in an uncharacteristic manner: "Wouldn't you think a death would relate to a life?" (*Box and Quotations*, 43). It is consonance she longs for; dissonance disturbs her.

The husband's death is analogous to the slow death of art and civilization that Voice grieves in *Box*. The Lady shares Voice's sense of loss, expressing her similar feeling most articulately in her painful memories of her daughter's behavior and the distance it has put between them. She recalls the night her daughter phoned to describe the Mexican boys she was in bed with at that moment:

I suppose that's why I came this time [on the voyage] . . . the Mexicans; the boys. Put an ocean between. (*Box and Quotations*, 56, 58)

Now she and her daughter "see each other less" (*Box and Quotations*, 54). Her husband's death and her daughter's decadence chart the decline of her own life. Her fall from the ship symbolizes her symbolic fall from grace and, in turn, represents the decline of the civilization she is part of.

At the end of her monologue, the Long-Winded Lady recalls the interrogation she underwent after she was pulled from the water (*Box and Quotations*, 67). The interrogators wanted to understand how she fell: Did she slip? Was she pushed? Had it happened before? This passage is the climactic moment in her narrative because it promises to answer the central mystery of her monologue, why she fell. It is the question she has been trying to answer throughout the play so she can resolve the dissonance of her experience. The repetition of themes in the speeches of the characters in *Quotations* and the juxtaposition of seemingly related passages suggest an implicit unity among the four monologues that the audience expects will become explicit. The audience, like the Lady's interrogators and the silent Minister, waits for her answer, the solution to Albee's puzzle. Why did she fall? No, she did not slip; no, she was not pushed. And of course it never happened before. After all is said, she has no explanation. Then she remembers them asking, "Do you think you may have done it on purpose? . . . Tried to kill yourself." After a "sad little half-laugh," she says, "Good heavens, no; I have nothing to die for" (*Box and Quotations*, 69–70).

This admission reveals to the audience the final, empty Chinese box, another box empty of promise and a life as bankrupt as the civilization that nurtured it. Her despair recalls the Old Woman's suffering—both have been rejected by their children—just as her disillusionment suggests the growing bitterness of Mao's final speeches. Her world is a microcosm of the larger worlds represented by the Old Woman and Mao. The themes of falling and dying resolve the dissonance created by Mao, the Old Woman, and Voice; this resolution is achieved by uniting the dissonant chords in a single melody, the Lady's disconsolate monologue.

Throughout *Quotations*, the Lady's struggle to understand her life is the only alternative to the fatalism and mechanical nature of Mao, the Old Woman, and the empty box on stage. *Quotations* creates much the same dichotomy between mechanical and human as *Play* does: the well-crafted, changeless box and the quoted texts of Mao and the Old Woman are opposed by the extemporaneous speeches of the Lady. She is not quoting, but inventing. She appears to be creating herself verbally, while Mao and the Old Woman are merely repeating themselves or others. The Lady and the Voice speak for the transitory nature of life, for change and adaptation, but the set texts of Mao and the Old Woman suggest the stasis physically embodied in the cube.

Since the Chairman advocates political change, it is ironic that his dogmatic thinking represents a threat to the Lady's struggle to change her own thinking, particularly her assumptions about cause and effect, the "fitness" of things, propriety—order. Her presumptions about the orderliness of life are continually being challenged by her disparate and confusing experiences. Consequently, her monologue questions her old sense of order and her search for a new one. Her self doubts and her perceptions of the world contrast with the arrogant certainty of Mao and the self-righteousness of the Old Woman. The Lady's soul-searching captures our sympathies, guides us through the confusing and conflicting experiences of the play, and finally permits us to hope for an answer to the play's puzzle in the Lady's quest to understand herself. It is painfully ironic for the audience that the Long-Winded Lady abandons her struggle to find meaning and consonance by saying she has "nothing to die for" and settling for the life of memories implicit in her statement, "My intention is only to remember" (Box and Quotations, 42).

Her admission that she has "nothing to die for" is the concluding line of Quotations, neatly juxtaposed against the first line of the "Reprise" of Box, in which Voice damns the Lady's selfishness by implication:

> When it was clear that we were not only corrupt . . . but corrupt to the selfishness, to the corruption that we should . . . go under rather than . . . (Box and Quotations, 71)

The thought proves too depressing to finish. Voice's phrase "go under" reminds us that the Lady's fall from the ship was the beginning of her metaphoric fall, her corruption. She has been so concerned with her fall, so self-absorbed, that she has been blind to the decline of society that Voice describes. Her selfishness is even more evident in her response to her husband's telling her he is dying: "But what about me! Think about me! (Box and Quotations, 50). Her inability to "contemplate anything . . . beyond a personal sense of loss," as Hayman puts it, has prevented her from noticing "the movement of our civilization towards holocaust.[23] In a sense, Mao is right when he suggests that the U.S. is doomed (Box and Quotations, 34). But it is not revolution that threatens American society, according to Albee, but an internal threat: the loss of a reason to live or die; the growing corruption; the realization, as Voice says, that "nothing belongs" (*Box and Quotations,* 73).

The Long-Winded Lady's resignation does not imply, as Donald Mullin argues, that life is meaningless.[24] Granted, by the end of *Quotations,* Mao, the Old Woman, and the Lady are boxed in by dogma, old age, and empty lives—a metaphor suggested by their silhouetted figures within the outline of the cube during the "Reprise" (*Box and Quotations,* 71). But the audience is not boxed in, although, as Cohn reminds us, "the threat is visually before us."[25] Albee's own remarks suggest a guarded optimism: "I *like* to think my plays are out to change people."[26] In his Introduction to the two plays, Albee says a playwright has two obligations:

> first, to make some statement about the condition of 'man' . . . and, second, to make some statement about the nature of the art form with which he is working. In both instances he must attempt change. In the first instance—since very few serious plays are written to glorify the status quo—the playwright must try to alter his society; in the second instance—since art must move, or wither—the playwright must try to alter the forms within which his precursors have had to work. (*Box and Quotations,* x)

Albee has altered the traditional dramatic form in much the same way Beckett did in *Play* and *Breath.* The separation of visual and acoustic space, and the consequent tension between the static box and the verbal struggles of the Long-Winded Lady and Voice to resist stasis and death, create a dissonance between sight and sound which, demanding resolution, thrusts the audience into the center of the dramatic conflict. Stated succinctly, "The play takes place in our heads."[27] Paolucci, describing the same phenomenon, says, "It is not what the [play] itself says but what you say to yourself when you hear it."[28] Albee's dissonant technique invites the audience to recreate the play in their own image, and to personalize the themes of decline and loss. Our role, then, is similar to Bigsby's description of that of the characters:

> brought together briefly in a constricted environment . . . they sit, uncommunicating, and reshape experience into maudlin entertainment, personal reminiscence, or political dogma.[29]

There is, however, an important difference between the audience and the characters: the characters are, as Paolucci suggests, trapped in their own consciousness,[30] but the audience is expected to transcend the limitations of all the Chinese boxes. Privy to the author's surrogate Voice, we are expected to heed the warning. We may refuse passage for the ship's journey—therein lies Albee's guarded optimism.

The ship within the cube symbolizes what David Higgens calls "mechanical, progressive, linear civilization, and . . . the rational, conscious mind, which works in terms of sequential time and linear space."[31] The box not only suggests the macrocosm of civilization and the microcosm of the mind; it also provides their connecting link, their linear nature. In other words, civilization's mechanical pursuit of progress results from the sequential nature of human rationality, and the corruption Voice warns us of is the penalty for our headlong rush forward.

Albee's experiment in musical structure, the counterpointing of monologues and sounding of thematic chords, gives new shape to an old message. Albee is serving in the time-honored role of artist as Early Warning System. "If only they had *told* us!" Voice complains. "When it was clear that we were . . . corrupt" (*Box* and *Quotations*, 71). Instead of telling us, which would make him guilty of the didacticism he parodies in Chairman Mao, Albee intends we suffer the decline of civilization and its arts ourselves. The dissonance his two inter-related plays create is meant to discomfort his audience, just as the beauty of the box "reminds us of *loss*" (*Box* and *Quotations*, 72). Measured against the tightly coherent structure of traditional drama and the expectations such orderly art fosters, the looser, fragmented structure of *Box* and *Quotations* may leave spectators at a loss—but not if we accept the work, as Voice suggests, "on its own terms" (*Box* and *Quotations*, 7). Then, freed from the restrictive boxes of convention and preconception, we can make the journey from "tension" (dissonance) to "tonic" (consonance) that Voice described in her initial monologue:

> The release of tension is the return to consonance; no matter how far traveled, one comes back, not circular, not to the starting point. . . . but a . . . setting down again, and the beauty of art is order—not what is familiar, necessarily, but order . . . on its own terms. (*Box* and *Quotations*, 7)

We do return, not to the starting point but to the "Reprise" of *Box* and Voice whispering in our ears, telling us of her vision of the birds, "a black net . . . skimming," and the lone bird, separate from the flock, like the artist from society, "moving . . . in the opposite way" (*Box* and *Quotations*, 74). The image, the speech, and the plays themselves invite us to join the Voice, the Lady, and the playwright in this search for a new principle of harmony.

4
Still Life:
Pinter's *Landscape* and *Silence*

"The only desperate conflict is between what we long to remember and what we need to forget."[1] The Long-Winded Lady's
remark identifies the implicit conflict between the two characters
in Harold Pinter's one-act play, *Landscape*: Beth remembers what
Duff has apparently forgotten, while Duff recalls what Beth
wishes to forget. This conflict remains implicit because *Landscape*, like *Play* and *Quotations*, is composed of discrete, intercut monologues. The lack of dialogue prevents the two characters
from confronting the other's contrary memories and emphasizes
the suggestive interplay of the tone, imagery, and intention of the
monologues. Furthermore, the stillness of the play's physical
space contrasts with its acoustic activity—similar to although
more muted than that in *Quotations*—thereby creating dissonance between sight and sound.

Beth, "a woman in her late forties," and Duff, "a man in his
early fifties,"[2] appear to be married, although this is never made
explicit. They live together in a country house, were hired as
caretakers of the house some time ago, and share a common past,
as Duff's monologue indicates. The play takes place in the
kitchen. The setting includes two chairs with a "long kitchen
table" between, and a dimly lit background of "a sink, stove, etc.,
and a window" (*Landscape*, 7). Neither Duff nor Beth moves
from the chair each sits in; in fact, no movement of any sort is
indicated in the script. Pinter's "Note" to the stage directions
says, "Beth never looks at Duff, and does not appear to hear his
voice" (*Landscape*, 7). Duff, however, "refers normally to Beth,"
although he too seems not to hear her speaking. It is as if Beth is
talking silently to herself so that Duff will not hear her and is
herself unable to hear him because of her internal monologue.

Such behavior is habitual for both of them, as Pinter implies in his description of the characters as "relaxed, in no sense rigid."

The importance of the play's setting is discounted by some critics, probably because of Pinter's extreme restrictions. Hayman describes the action of Landscape as consisting "entirely of words and sounds."[3] Similarly, Austin E. Quigley says that "only verbal activity occurs."[4] Technically, both are wrong: Beth and Duff are both allowed a full range of facial expressions, unlike the urn characters in Play; and Duff repeatedly directs his words, and presumably his face or head, toward Beth. Although these motions are limited, they are extremely important, because the characters' body postures reveal a great deal about their relation to one another. Pinter specifically directs that Beth never look at Duff and that Duff refer to her normally, conferring significance upon as mundane an activity as looking at the person being addressed. Beth does not look at Duff, indicating the degree to which she lives in a world separate from his. Her interior monologue is composed largely of memories; his monologue, addressed mainly to her, resembles the conversation of a husband telling his wife the day's events. However, the verbal isolation created by the lack of dialogue and by the different qualities of the monologues is opposed by the visual fact of their simultaneous presence in the same space. Simon Trussler understates the case when he says,

> It is helpful . . . to know that the play's only two characters . . . actually are sitting together in the same room, and not merely voices or memories alternating or occasionally—almost—communicating in some limbo of lost memories.[5]

It is essential to notice that the characters are in the same kitchen, because the play makes it apparent immediately how separate they are.

In a sense, Landscape includes three spaces: his, hers, and theirs. His and her places in the kitchen are visually separated by the long table that stands conspicuously empty between them. Acoustically their two places are distinguished by their very different monologues. The kitchen itself suggests the third place—theirs—locating Duff and Beth in a concrete present that contrasts with the fictionalized pasts they fabricate in their monologues. Ironically, they share nothing in this third space except physical proximity. Typical associations with a kitchen setting, e.g., a family nourished by conversation and food, are contradicted by the verbal separateness of Duff and Beth. Their joint physical presence in the same room underscores the absence of dialogue and heightens the audience's perception of their isolation from one another. Therefore, place is crucial in drawing the audience's attention to the disjunction of the characters' verbal separation and visual conjunction.

Landscape's verbal space is charged with the tension implicit in the variant content and styles of the two monologues; visual space, according to Pinter's directions, is relaxed. Thus, dissonance is experienced at three levels: aurally, in the opposition of the two intercut monologues; visually, in the reversal of audience associations with the familiar setting; and cognitively, in the incongruity of the audience's aural and visual experiences. The audience's struggle to resolve dissonance unites the play's fragmentary structure and, therefore, is the central dramatic action.

Beth's monologue is a lyrical stream-of-consciousness recollection of a romantic time at the beach with an unidentified man. It contrasts sharply with Duff's prosaic telling of what he did that day. She neither hears him nor speaks to him, but is lost in revery. Her monologue centers on two images: the "desolate" beach where she used to go with "my man" (Landscape, 9); and his touch, which she compares to the "light, delicate" touch of the waves (Landscape, 16). She moves from the idyllic memory of the beach and the man's touch to other concerns that diminish the sweetness of her memory—to an old man far away on the horizon of the beach (Landscape, 13, 17), to women who seem to be watching her (Landscape, 9, 10, 11), and to her discovery that "there was nothing to draw. Only the beach, the sea" (Landscape, 18). But she always returns to her memory of the man's touch, as if to escape the other, less-than-perfect memories. She describes how he touched the back of her neck lightly (Landscape, 13, 18), put his arms around her (Landscape, 20), and cuddled her (Landscape, 21). She tries to recreate the special feeling of being alone with him on an empty beach and to experience his tenderness, but other memories intrude and threaten the feeling, memories of other people on the beach or of certain moments when, for some inexplicable reason, they cannot or will not touch: "I lay by him, not touching" (*Landscape*, 11). At those moments, she is afraid she will spoil the mood by saying or doing something that will upset him, something she implies she has done before: "But I wasn't a fool, on that occasion. I lay quiet, by his side" (*Landscape*, 14). These memories intrude on her romantic recollections of "my man" and remind her of some unexpressed lack in their relationship, an emotional distance ironically contrasted with their physical closeness—a prefiguring of her relation to Duff. The emotional distance between Beth and her man at the beach is symbolized by the drawing she made in the sand:

> I drew a face in the sand, then a body. The body of a woman. Then the body of a man, close to her, not touching. But they didn't look like anything. They didn't look like human figures. The sand kept slipping, mixing the contours. I crept close to him and put my head on his arm, and closed my eyes. . . . I buried my face in his side and shut the light out. (*Landscape*, 20)

She senses something unreal in her relation with the man, which is why her figures do not look human, and the sensation frightens her. The landscape of her memory keeps slipping, like the sand, so she uses him to shield her from the light of that realization.

Although Pinter never states that she fears something or what that something may be, it is implied by the juxtaposing of Duff's and Beth's monologues. Duff's physical presence on stage, coupled with the manner in which his speeches are interspersed between Beth's, leads the audience to search for connections. At times their words do seem to touch as their separate consciousnesses "brush as gently as shadows intercepting."[6] Occasionally they seem to echo one another, as when Duff describes the empty park he walked in that afternoon—"There wasn't a soul in the park"—and Beth's next speech describes the empty beach in exactly the same words, "There wasn't a soul on the beach" (*Landscape*, 13); or when Beth's memory of being at a bar with her man is juxtaposed with Duff's story about the argument he had at the pub that afternoon (*Landscape*, 25–27). More often, however, Duff hints about what might keep them living in the same house, if not exactly together, in spite of the isolation and tension the audience so palpably discerns. He reminds her she was a first-rate housekeeper for Mr. Sykes, the man who owns the country estate they now occupy. Although Beth is not listening and has never indicated to him that she might be, Duff suggests cleaning the place up. (Sykes has apparently left the house to them; it is unclear whether he is dead or simply absent.) Then in two successive speeches Duff suggests how their present distant relationship may have evolved. He says he is pleased that she no longer "nag[s] the shit out of [him]" yet in his next line asserts that "what matters" is that they are still together (Landscape, 24). Apparently her withdrawal pleases him because she no longer nags him; he can feel satisfied that they have stayed together and that he has someone he can talk to without having to accommodate himself to her. He doesn't even have to listen to her.

Their separation, then, is more temporal than physical. Although they never approach one another on stage, their presence in the kitchen contrasts with the different time frames of their monologues. Duff speaks primarily of the present or the immediate past of that day's events; Beth speaks only of a distant past, perhaps fantasized but certainly romanticized. Duff fantasizes, too, but it is not evident to the audience until his final speech. The realistic, mundane details of his day, especially when contrasted with Beth's idyllic recollections, give credence to the reality of his memory. The audience believes his description is accurate, because there is no reason to believe otherwise, until his final, bizarre speech.

There is one moment when Beth's memory seems to jog Duff's, as if he hears her in spite of Pinter's directions. She describes an autumn morning when she looked out the window and watched children in the misty valley below. Duff's following speech begins:

> I never saw your face. You were standing by the windows. One of those black nights. . . . You knew I'd come in but you didn't move. . . . Perhaps you were just thinking, in a dream. (Landscape, 27)

Although the difference in time of day in their recollections seems to indicate two different events, it is not certain, especially because memory plays tricks on Pinter's characters; and Duff or Beth or both may have misremembered the same incident. The passage further contrasts their separation in time with their conjunction in space at the same window. The juxtaposition of the two speeches, therefore, suggests that their present emotional distance was evident much earlier; Beth may have been daydreaming and carrying on internal monologues for years. She is clearly trying to escape Duff's presence, which is suggested by this passage as well as by the technique of juxtaposing her internal monologue with Duff's remarks to her. Although the audience may want to jump to the conclusion that the unnamed man in Beth's fantasy/memory is the young Duff, she is obviously excluding Duff by focusing on a romance at the beach. Early in the play she recalls how the men in her life held her arm "lightly" as she got out of cars. "Without exception. If they touched the back of my neck . . . it was done so lightly. Without exception. With one exception" (*Landscape*, 12). That exception is Duff. The crudeness of his following speech—"mind you, there was a lot of shit all over the place"—is juxtaposed against her delicacy. Later he recalls the day he returned from a trip to tell her he had been unfaithful (*Landscape*, 19). He stresses how gentle he was to her, as if such gentleness were unusual and therefore worthy of particular notice: "I was very gentle to you. I was kind to you, that day. I knew you'd had a shock, so I was gentle with you" (*Landscape*, 22).

The conversational tone of Duff's monologue contrasts with Beth's personal revery. He repeatedly tries to include her in his speeches: "The dog's gone. I didn't tell you"; "You should have a walk with me one day down to the pond, bring some bread. There's nothing to stop you"; "I've put in some flowers. You'd find it pleasant" (*Landscape*, 10, 12, 16). He seems compelled to justify his talking as something she enjoys in spite of her lack of response:

> Do you like me to talk to you? [Pause.] Do you like me to tell you about all the things I've been doing? [Pause.] I think you do. (*Landscape*, 21)

On one hand, Duff's inclusion of Beth in his comments and thoughts is a generous act that contrasts with her selfish, preoccupied monologue and belies the violence he expresses later toward her. On the other hand, his references and questions to her may merely be habitual or a contrivance to maintain the illusion of normality.

Beth's monologue is more self-sustaining than Duff's. She does not need to justify herself in terms of Duff or anyone else. Her speech is unsocial and onanistic. The landscape of the play's title is the landscape of Beth's mind, remembering and distorting the past. Duff is an intruder in her territory. Her speeches are lyric, his are prosaic; when she is gentle, he is coarse. She lives in the past, and he tries to bring her into the present by describing his daily activities. Duff emphasizes the "potential closeness" of their relationship, evident in their positioning on stage, by including Beth in his thoughts and plans and by asserting, "We're together. That's what matters" (Landscape, 24). Yet Beth's oblivious stance denies his assertion. She avoids the coarser aspects of life that Duff embodies—the "dogshit, duckshit . . . all kinds of shit" (Landscape, 12) he talks about. She wants to remember only the lovely, delicate things in her life, particularly those associated with her man on the beach:

> the lightness of your touch, the lightness of your look, my neck, your eyes, the silence, that is my meaning, the loveliness of my flowers, my hands touching my flowers, that is my meaning. (Landscape, 24)

Beth's idealized pictures contrast with Duff's crude actions,[7] and this tension is most evident in the concluding passages of Landscape, in which Beth returns to her memories of her beach romance while Duff's speeches grow increasingly violent. Her monologue is cyclical, beginning with the images surrounding her man and the beach and proceeding through a series of related images, each one diminishing her memory of the beach idyll. The last of these troubling memories is an incident at the beach that nearly caused her, as she says, to lose heart (Landscape, 28). She asked her man to turn and look at her, but when he did she could not see his look because his face was in shadow (Landscape, 28–29). This recollection so disturbs her that she returns immediately to the memory she had at the play's beginning— alone with the man at the beach—thus completing a cycle of idyllic revery, memories interrupting revery, and return to revery.

In the meantime, Duff concludes his story about the debate at the pub over how draught beer is stored with a description of tapping a beer cask. His imagery is startlingly sexual and foreshadows the sexual violence of his final speech. The bung he refers to is the stopper plugging the opening of the cask; but "bung" also means "asshole," making the speech suggestive of anal intercourse or rape.

> The bung is on the vertical, in the bunghole. Spile the bung. Hammer the spile through the centre of the bung. . . . Then you hammer the tap in. (*Landscape*, 25)

He continues suggestively, although gentler in tone, as he recalls standing behind Beth watching her figure in the dark window:

> I stood close to you. Perhaps you were just thinking, in a dream. Without touching you, I could feel your bottom. (*Landscape*, 27)

This speech echoes Beth's references to lying next to her man without touching (*Landscape*, 11, 13) and to her drawing in the sand, but with a foreboding difference. There is a threat implicit in Duff's "without touching you, I could feel your bottom" that is realized in the increasingly violent imagery of his subsequent speeches. His escalating, aggressive language is counterpointed by Beth's retreat into fantasy and memory.

Duff's final speech, like Beth's, is probably a mixture of fact and fantasy. He recalls the chain and thimble she wore around her waist when she would stand in the hall and bang the gong, presumably to signal mealtime:

> What the bloody hell are you doing banging that bloody gong? . . . It's bullshit. . . . There's no one to listen. No one'll hear. There's not a soul in the house. Except me. There's nothing cooked. No stew. No pie. No greens. No joint. Fuck all. (*Landscape*, 28)

He then describes taking the chain and thimble off her, booting the gong down the hall, and expecting her to come to him and offer herself. "I would have had you in front of the dog, like a man, in the hall, on the stone, banging the gong" (*Landscape*, 29). His fantasy of having her while banging the gong rises to a crescendo of violence—"bang your lovely head, mind the dog doesn't swallow the thimble, slam"—and is suddenly cut off. After a silence, Beth's closing images of the tender touch and kiss of her man, the sweet sensation of the sand on her skin, and the

silence of the sky resemble a litany sung to ward off the disturbing shadows Duff cast on her memory.

If Duff's sexual fantasy is rape-like, Beth's is masturbatory. Her
sensuous imagery, especially the autoeroticism of "my hands
touching my flowers" (Landscape, 24), is appropriately onanistic
and contrasts vividly with Duff's imaginary violation of her. But
Duff's physical immobility contrasts markedly with the violence
of his final speech. His rape is unfulfilled: he never moves from
his chair, nor does he display physical tension. The usual coherence of verbal and visual media that shapes an audience's
expectation that violent language will be accompanied by action
is sundered by the dissonant coupling of Duff's violent imagery
and staccato rhythms in his last speech with his immobility. As
already seen in Play and Quotations, verbal space is filled wit'
the noise of activity while visual space remains static. Stephen
Martineau has coined the oxymoron "still violence"[8] to describe
the central discord of Landscape. The central conflict of Landscape is not a struggle between the characters, as some critics
have suggested;[9] it is the dissonant juxtaposition of verbal violence and visual stillness. Duff and Beth are not at a standoff,
which implies impending confrontation, but a standstill. His
coarse day-to-day activity exists side-by-side with, although not
touching, her delicate fantasies. Their potential actions, Duff's
desire to bang Beth and her unstated wish to leave him, are
immobilized by their internal conflicts, which the audience perceives as a dichotomy of verbal activity and visual stasis.

Landscape takes place in the aftermath of the kind of conflict
that usually energizes a play. Whatever battle Duff and Beth
fought to arrive at their present tolerance for and exclusion of one
another happened long ago. The play begins with conventional
dramatic action already arrested. The dramatic situation, John
Russell Brown points out, is static, "as if energies have reached a
point of balance or exhaustion."[10] Beth and Duff appear resigned
to and comfortable in their situation. Beth is undisturbed by
Duff's noisy presence; she lingers in her revery as long as she can
avoid unpleasant memories. Although Duff's violent speeches
may result from his frustration at not being able to reach Beth
anymore, literally or metaphorically, the frustration is not great
enough to compel him to take physical action. He even reminds
himself of the advantages of their present relationship: "At least

now, I can walk down to the pub in peace and up to the pond in peace, with no-one to nag the shit out of me" (*Landscape*, 24).

Inter-character conflict has been shifted in *Landscape*, in Francis Gillens' words, "from the external arena where it had been dramatized through actions and dialogue which were taking place outside the mind, into the mind itself."[11] The play's physical setting may be a kitchen, but its metaphoric setting is the landscapes of the minds of its two characters. The play's conflict lies within each inscape rather than between them. Duff and Beth are immobilized by an internal division between their remembered pasts and their present, between the fantasies they create and the reality that intrudes as disruptive memories. This internal division is conveyed to the audience through the polarization of sound and sight: the characters' histories, and their fabrications of such, are spoken, while their present reality is conveyed primarily through light. This disjunction of memory and current situation is experienced by the audience as a disjunction of the verbal and visual media.

Beth tries to reduce her internal conflict between "What we long to remember and what we need to forget" (as Albee's Voice describes it) by recasting her memories to fit how she thinks it should have been, or how she wants it to be, and by avoiding memories that contradict or diminish her fantasies. Her withdrawal from the present stalemates Duff's attempts to include her in his life. Although we might expect them eventually to cease all verbal activity and retreat into the silence of internal monologue, especially when we consider that their "relaxed" manner and tone imply that their exhaustive condition is not unusual, they persist in talking despite the futility of words. In so doing they exhibit a behavior common to the characters in *Play* and *Quotations*, what Quigley calls "avoidance of silence."[12]

The characters in *Landscape*'s twin one-act play, *Silence*, also refuse to be silent in spite of a multitude of circumstances: their isolation from one another, the disparity between their words and acts, the pointlessness of speech, and the title of the play itself. For some unexpressed reason, they must speak. Like *Landscape*, *Silence* is informed by the dichotomy of static visual and dynamic verbal. Neither play explains why its characters tolerate such dissonance. Both plays leave the audience, as Quigley observes, "with the knowledge that final knowledge is never achieved."[13]

In both the London and New York productions, *Silence* was performed on the same bill with *Landscape* in an arrangement similar to that of Albee's *Box-Mao-Box:* first *Silence* was performed in its entirety, then *Landscape,* then *Silence* again.[14] Nena Thames Whittemore suggests that the trio of plays mirrors the trio of lovers; that the three characters in *Silence,* a woman and two men, are manifestations of the three in *Landscape,* Duff, Beth, and her unnamed man.[15] The *Silence* characters—Ellen, Rumsey, and Bates—also share a common past that is revealed through intercut monologues and a few brief dialogues. However, *Silence* is told from three points of view and from two separate points in time.[16] The disparity between the different time periods is the major source of dissonance in the play, because while both time frames are represented verbally only one is represented visually. Visual time, as evident in the physical age of the characters, is contradicted repeatedly by verbal time as revealed in the monologues. Pinter's character descriptions specify that Ellen is "a girl in her twenties," Rumsey "a man of forty," and Bates "in his middle thirties" (*Landscape,* 31). Yet both Ellen and Bates speak most of their monologues from the point of view and point in time of very old people recalling their distant, younger years.

Bates, for example, remembers being called "Grandad" by the noisy kids whose music disturbs his sleep; he threatens them, saying, "Were I young . . ." (*Landscape,* 35). Later he relates a "stupid conversation" with his landlady during which she accuses him of being "a childish old man" (*Landscape,* 43). Once he had a little girl whom he took for walks, but now he lives alone, bitter about the solitude of his old age: "having no solace, no constant solace, not even any damn inconstant solace" (*Landscape,* 36). Such statements are incongruous coming from the thirty-year-old man seen on stage. Their incongruity is underlined by several passages that indicate a much younger man is speaking, passages consistent with Bates's physical age. For example, he describes taking a woman (Ellen) to his cousin's place in town and seducing her (*Landscape,* 34)—a direct contradiction of his complaint about no "damn inconstant solace." His brief dialogue with Ellen further suggests he is speaking from two distant points in time, because he tries to persuade her to meet with him that night to go to his cousin's place in town (*Landscape*, 37). Although their dialogue is in the present tense, he has already described the outcome of that meeting, the seduction. The conflicting evidence of Bates's present age and of the memories implying he is much older is dramatized by the disjunction of his physical and verbal ages.

Interestingly, no such ambiguity surrounds the character of Rumsey. His speeches lack specific time references, but they are compatible with his given age of forty, perhaps to indicate his satisfaction with his solitary life: "Pleasant alone" (*Landscape*, 35).

Rumsey's sensitivity is contrasted with Bates's latent violence. Bates speaks of "bumping lights," "cars barking," "pissing dark," and uses verbs like "smack," "clutch," and "clench" (*Landscape*, 34). Rumsey, however, has vivid memories of walking with Ellen (*Landscape*, 33) and a very lyrical, sensuous recollection of Ellen "floating . . . under me" (*Landscape*, 40). In the dialogue between Rumsey and Ellen, there is no tension; they share pleasant memories, and she agrees to cook for him on her next visit (*Landscape*, 41–42). Between Bates and Ellen, however, there is a struggle: he tries to persuade her to meet with him that night, but she resists (*Landscape*, 37–39). According to Bates, when he and Ellen do meet, he "press[es] the smile off [her] face" (*Landscape*, 35). The contrast between Rumsey and Bates is similar to that between Beth and Duff: one character associated with tenderness, the other with roughness.

Yet Bates longs to be like Rumsey. He envies Rumsey his life in the country; he wants to escape the worry and bustle of his city life. He repeats a conversation he once had with his little girl about a bird she saw in a tree, a speech that reveals his longing for the simple, peaceful existence he attributes to animals:

> Birds grow tired, after they've flown over the country, up and down in the wind, looking down on all the sights, so sometimes, when they reach a tree, with good solid branches, they rest. (*Landscape*, 40)

Bates has rested only on rare occasions, and the experience remains strange to him:

> Sometimes I press my hand on my forehead, calmingly, feel all the dust drain out, let it go, feel the grit slip away. Funny moment. That calm moment. (*Landscape*, 41)

Now he wants his life to be filled with such moments, as he imagines Rumsey's is. Bates yearns for a life in which, as Rumsey puts it, "there is no-one to tell me what is expected of me . . . nothing required of me" (Landscape, 35). The line echoes the sentiment expressed by Duff in his line, "no-one to nag the shit out of me." This wish unites the three men, although Rumsey is the only one to achieve it. He has retreated from life to live alone with his animals and memories; Bates merely dreams of such an existence. (And Duff, in spite of no longer being nagged by Beth, is still justifying his behavior to her as if she were nagging.) Whether the change is realized or still desired, the movement away from the conflicts and tensions inevitable in any human relationship and toward the calm that comes from the absence of the expectations of others—a retreat embodied in its extreme by Beth's solipsism—parallels the audience's movement from dissonance to consonance, which is likewise a release from tension and a resolution of expectations.

Ellen's relation to each man highlights their differences. She links them metaphorically and literally, verbally and visually. Pinter has isolated Bates, Rumsey, and Ellen in three separate areas on stage. There is no set, just a chair in each pool of light (Landscape, 31), and darkness surrounds and separates each of them. During their brief passages of dialogue, however, one character joins another in his or her space. Bates moves to Ellen once, and Ellen moves to Rumsey twice. She provides a visual link between the two men. Rumsey never moves, which further characterizes his passive, self-satisfied nature and distinguishes him from Bates. Yet Ellen's recollections of being with them together—as well as her obvious fondness for both—stress the similarity of their experiences with her: "There are two. . . . I kiss them there. . . . I look away to smile, and touch them as I turn" (Landscape, 35).

Ellen's memories imply a woman much older than the "girl in her twenties" Pinter's description indicates. Her ambiguous age focuses the dissonance between the visual and verbal not only because her words contradict her physical age, as was the case with Bates, but also because she articulates an ambivalence about her age that heightens the audience's awareness of the discord. She relates a conversation she had with her "drinking companion" about what she calls "my early life, when I was young"

(*Landscape*, 36). Ellen tells her elderly lady friend, "I'm old, . . . my youth was somewhere else, anyway I don't remember." Later she adds, "I seem to be old" (*Landscape*, 43). Yet near the end of the play she seems less certain whether she is old or not: "I'm never sure that what I remember is of to-day or of yesterday or of a long time ago" (*Landscape*, 46). The audience shares this uncertainty.

The ambiguity of the characters' ages is complemented by the indefinite space the play takes place in. *Landscape's* kitchen setting creates a specific and definite here and now for the action, but the lack of details of setting in *Silence* creates an indefinite space, a nowhere in which time cannot be specified. Past and present are often indistinguishable. Consequently, there is no discernible movement in time, neither forward nor backward nor circular; neither is there plot development, because that requires a linear notion of time. Finally, there can be no measurable change in character where there is no identifiable past to measure such change against. *Silence*, however, is not entirely static. There remains a slight movement, a deterioration, a settling into the still life the play anticipates.

Ellen most clearly charts the play's movement toward that final silence, the complete breakdown of communication. Her dialogues with each of the men and her memories of the three of them together imply a community that contrasts with their physical isolation on stage as well as with their statements about solitude in their old age. Something drove them apart, however, something that occurred between the time they were together, represented by their physical ages and brief dialogues, and the present in which they live alone in their memories. Pinter, as usual, offers no explicit explanations of his characters' histories; however, there is a hint in Ellen's recollection of a "wind . . . so high" that one of the men does not hear her (*Landscape*, 34). The event is never developed, but it suggests that when one of the men failed to hear her, it may have sown the seeds for their final isolation. This failure to hear is reiterated in a passage in which Rumsey's and Bates's memories seem to converge:

Rumsey. She was looking down. I couldn't hear what she said.
Bates.   I can't hear you [she said]. Yes you can, I said.
Rumsey. What are you saying? Look at me, she said.

Bates.   I didn't. I didn't hear you, she said. I didn't hear what you
said.
Rumsey.   But I am looking at you. It's your head that's bent. (Landscape, 43–44)

Rumsey remembers not hearing Ellen because she had her face
turned away; Bates recalls Ellen not hearing him. The failure to
hear parallels Beth's failure to see her lover's face; each act—
hearing and seeing—is appropriate to the particular play, Silence
and Landscape.

The similarity of the men's experiences reminds us of the trio's
closeness, how much their lives touched one another. Yet, ironically, the counterpointing of the men's memories underscores
the essential separation of character. Both men speak of the
difficulties of communicating, yet they do so unaware of one
another, locked into their own monologues. The structure of the
passage, the intercut monologues touching in substance yet separate in fact, is a perfect analogue for the subject of the passage.
The echo of dialogue—at times it is almost as if they are speaking
to each other—heightens our awareness of their loneliness and
suggests the deterioration of their community. Speech often
works this way in Pinter's plays, as an indication of the distance
between characters rather than as a bridge spanning the gulf.
What takes place in speech, Pinter says, "is a continual evasion,
desperate rearguard attempts to keep ourselves to ourselves.
Communicating is too alarming."[17] Even in speech we isolate
ourselves.

Rumsey's solitary life and Bates's desire for rest and quiet are
manifestations of the wish to be left alone. Ellen's attitude, however, is more ambivalent. Her physical isolation on stage is coun-
tered by remarks that show her need for companionship.
Although she says, "After my work each day I walk back through
people but I don't notice them" (Landscape, 46), she also expresses a need for someone to listen to her and help her understand herself: "Am I old now? No-one will tell me. I must find a
person to tell me these things" (Landscape, 43).

But the silence increases despite her need to talk and listen.
She equates the growing silence with the darkness surrounding
her, and both become metaphors of her old age and imminent
death:

Around me sits the night. Such a silence. . . . As my eyes close I see last of lights far over black across black under my eyes far away lights over hills closing. (*Landscape*, 43, 46)

The broken syntax of the speech suggests the breakdown in communication among the three characters. It occurs immediately before the closing section of the play, which is a reprise that consists of fragmented lines of earlier monologues repeated much in the manner of Voice's reprise of *Box*. The number of silences between speeches increases until at the end every line is punctuated by a silence (*Landscape*, 49–52). And so the play moves inexorably toward fulfilling its title. The final tableau, a "long silence" as the audience joins Ellen in watching the light fade to black, is a still-life portrait.

Duff's "still violence" at the end of *Landscape* is transformed into the utter stillness of the ensuing dark Ellen describes in *Silence*. Both plays, then, are landscapes of the human mind, explorations of the silence behind words and the empty spaces in human consciousness. In *Silence* the characters are isolated in space, yet their memories touch the same points in time. *Landscape*'s characters share the same space but are isolated in time. In both plays, the disjunction of time and space replaces the traditional conflict between characters. In *Landscape* the dissonance results from the incongruity of the verbal activity of Duff and Beth and the visually static quality of the play; in *Silence*, on the other hand, dissonance results from discrepancies between visual and verbal implications of time. Because the audience perceives the discontinuous relation of sight and sound, the central conflict of each play is transferred from the stage to the spectators. The audience must resolve the conflicts the plays create. John Lahr describes how this works for *Landscape*, and his description serves for *Silence*, too:

Pinter forces the audience toward the center of his drama, denying their position outside the conflict. Crammed close to the stage image, the audience can be inundated with stimuli without having the final say on the experience, without being able to make "sense" of it.[18]

The themes of the isolation of the individual and the dissolution of love bonds are common to both plays, as are the techniques used to dramatize them. Both the fragmentation of monologues and the separation of verbal and visual media suggest each person's ineluctable "aloneness." In *Silence*, the dissolution of language and memory is a metaphor for the crumbling social bonds that keep us together in spite of our isolation. Pinter's characters are as lonely and immobile as Beckett's are in their urns. They are, says James R. Hollis, "alone as they had always been alone."[19]

All of Beckett's, Albee's, and Pinter's characters live in a prison of memories. Bates most clearly articulates this confinement of the individual within the self when he says, "I walk in my mind. But can't get out of the walls" (*Landscape*, 39). The landscape of the mind is a trap.

5
Theatre of the Mind

"Drama," Friedrich Dürrenmatt wrote, "can dupe the spectator into exposing himself to reality."[1] Each theatrical movement during this century—realism, surrealism, expressionism, absurdism—has exploited a different technique for duping audiences. The polarization of the visual and verbal media, a recent innovation, dramatically alters the typically passive role of the audience removed from the play's action. It creates dissonance between the play's media and requires the spectator to resolve the dissonance or feel cheated of meaning. In the theatre of discord, therefore, it is the audience, not the characters, who are the protagonists: we alone feel the conflict created by the separation of sight and sound. The playwright, then, becomes our antagonist, provoking our response by fragmenting our experience. The opposition of light and sound in *Play*, the isolation of monologues in *Quotations*, and the contradiction of frenzied word and static actor in *Landscape* do not resolve by play's end into a coherent world portrait. Their discord parallels the jangle of experiences we call living, just as the patternless chaos of lines and colors in abstract expressionistic painting or the clash of disharmonious sounds in avant-garde music are both consequences and representations of the confusion of modern life.

The struggle facing the contemporary artist, according to Beckett, is to find a form capable of accommodating the confusing data of experience, what he calls "the mess." Traditionally, art has imposed form upon chaotic experience; but Beckett believes are can no longer withhold "the mess." This does not mean art will become formless; rather, Beckett explains,

> there will be new form . . . of such a type that it admits the chaos and does not try to say that the chaos is really something else. . . . To find a form that accommodates the mess, that is the task of the artist now.[2]

69

Beckett has persisted in his search for a new form. In *Not I*
(1972), the separation of the verbal from the visual is graphically
represented by Mouth—suspended in the darkness, the sole
source of sound—and the silent, hooded figure on the opposite
side of the stage.[3] Like the urn characters, Mouth is a disembodied voice. Yet the dismemberment is more complete in *Not I*;
even the face has vanished, only the Mouth remains. The silent
figure reminds us of the once united body and the harmony of its
parts, now fragmented and isolated.

Whether he restricts his characters to urns, as in *Play*, or limits
his drama to an incessant stream of words punctuated by four
gestures of "helpless compassion" made by the cloaked figure, as
in *Not I*, Beckett replaces the traditional inter-character conflict
with tension between the frenzied activity of speech and the
impossibility of movement. In *Footfalls* (1977), a woman (May)
paces back and forth the length of a narrow strip of light while
conversing with a voice from the surrounding darkness.[4] Verbally, she is coming to terms with her past, much as Albee's
Long-Winded Lady does, so she can escape the burden of one
mysterious experience. But May can no more escape her past and
these repetitive musings about it than she can walk beyond the
strip of light. She is imprisoned by both; the audience, however,
feels the tension between the implied release of language—the
freedom that confession and explanation supposedly bring—and
the absolute prison of light. Her relation to the strip of light is
similar to that of the urn characters to the spotlight. This battle of
lights and voices also occurs in *That Time* (1977), in which the
frenzied language spoken by three disembodied voices is pitched
against the immobile face of the Listener.[5]

Pinter and Albee have been less persistent than Beckett in their
experiments with dissonant drama. Their brief ventures into this
type of theatre probably result from their admiration for Beckett's
work: both have paid public tribute to him and his influence on
their work.[6] However, both have returned to more traditional
forms after their experiments with dissonant theatre. *Box* and
Quotations are Albee's only ventures into the theatre of discord
to date. Pinter followed the one-act plays *Landscape* and *Silence*
with a full-length play, *Old Times* (1971), which integrates dissonant techniques with realistic conventions, especially within a
realistic setting. The play takes place in a naturalistic interior

setting without the intercut monologues of the previous one-act plays. All preconceptions are shattered, however, by Anna's presence in the room during Kate's and Deeley's discussion of her *anticipated* arrival. They speak as though she were not there, with the same absence of awareness of others on stage found in *Landscape* and *Silence:*

> *Deeley.*   Was she your best friend?
> *Kate.*   Oh, what does that mean? . . .
> *Deeley.*   Can't you remember what you felt?
> Pause.
> *Kate.*   It is a very long time.
> *Deeley.*   But you remember her. She remembers you. Or why would
> she be coming here tonight?[7]

Throughout the extensive discussion of Anna's arrival that follows, the audience can plainly see Anna standing behind Deeley and Kate. The discord created by visual information that blatantly contradicts the verbal content echoes throughout the play, altering the play's tone, making it more mysterious and unsettling. *Old Times* does not take the radical form of Beckett's later work, but it suggests one way in which dissonant structures may be adapted to more conventional dramas.

The theatre of discord is quite naturally preoccupied with perception, given its technique of polarizing the audience's two modes of perceiving. In their characters' struggles to accommodate the confusion of their lives, these plays reflect the audience's parallel struggle to assimilate the dissonant experience of the plays themselves. The urn characters, the Long-Winded Lady, Duff and Beth, and the trio in *Silence* all tell and retell their experiences, hoping to make sense of them, assimilate them, fit them into the patterns of their lives. On the other side of the stage lights, we in the audience mimic the characters' behavior, recalling details from the plays, perhaps remembering similar personal experiences as we too search for patterns, order, meaning. We take part in a drama larger than the one on stage, a theatre of memory. Just as the Long-Winded Lady remembers her dissonant experience coming out of the bakery into the midst of a taxi accident—first thinking that a movie was being made, later realizing what happened, and finally looking for the words to tell about it—so we in the audience re-member these plays at a later time, rearranging their dissonant parts, searching for that elusive pattern that will bring it all together. We are like May in Beckett's *Footfalls*, pacing back and forth repeating the same con- versations, recalling the same experiences. A voice asks her, "Will you never have done? . . . Will you never have done . . . revolving it all? . . . In your poor mind." (*Footfalls*, 13). Although our pacing is entirely cerebral, we too are trapped in a prison of language and memory, doomed to revolve it all in the endless struggle to accommodate the mess.

The role of the spectator in dissonant theatre is similar to the one Bernard Baschet sees for the contemporary artist: "to seek a certain order which coincides in the space without and the space within."[8] One of the contributions of the Absurdists, Esslin sug- gests, was to develop "a stage convention capable of putting on to the stage an *internal psychological* reality, an inscape of the mind."[9] The theatre of discord expands that convention, follow- ing Beckett's suggestion that

> the only fertile research is excavatory, immersive, a contraction of the spirit, a descent. The artist is active, but negatively, shrinking from the nullity of extracircumferential phenomena, drawn in to the core of the eddy.[10]

For some time, Beckett has been the guiding presence in this theatre turned inward. His setting for *Endgame*, a room resem- bling the interior of a skull,[11] was an early example of the play's action as metaphor for the brain's activity. His more recent plays, particularly *Not I*, *That Time*, and *Footfalls*, are composed almost exclusively of internal monologues.

Beckett's journey inward is paralleled by Albee's efforts to locate the Voice of *Box* in the minds of the audience and by Pinter's use of internal monologues. Ellen, in *Silence*, sounds like an urn character consumed in self-contemplation when she says, "I sometimes wonder if I think. I heard somewhere about how many thoughts go through the brain of a person. But I couldn't remember anything I'd actually thought."[12]

Ellen's paradoxical inability to remember her thoughts in the midst of her memory-filled monologue typifies the landscape of the mind-at-work that these playwrights paint. Logical connec- tions are replaced by associative ones; linear structures of action and time give way to circular motions around a static center; and monologue takes the place of dialogue. Lack of a conventional plot with its rising action and climax, as well as the intentionally ambiguous representation of time that characterizes these plays, suggest that Beckett, Albee, and Pinter find the principle of cause and effect, which informs the conventional plot, and the notion of linear time to be inappropriate models for representing the mind's processes. Beth's statement that "The cause of the shadow cannot be found" (Landscape, 28) suggests that although we may know effects, causes are often unknowable. This is not to say that Western civilization as a whole has rejected the notions of cause and effect or linear time; yet three major dramatists feel a need to create new metaphors and analogies for describing our perception and assimilation of experience. That is noteworthy. "Artists," Ezra Pound reminds us, "are the antennae of the race."[13]

Dramatic structure, according to Jackson G. Berry, "must move always forward, the way we assume man's life moves forward in a pattern of time set on its one-directional course."[14] Berry's assumptions about dramatic structure and time may be appropriate for traditional drama, but not for a theatre of discord. Berry hypothesizes that if our civilization comes to see cause and effect as an illusion, drama will "assume a form more closely allied to the repetitive form in music"; and these plays do seem to fulfill Walter Pater's dictum that "art constantly aspires towards the condition of music."[15] Linear time is violated by the fusion of past and present in both Play and Silence, resulting in a structure that returns upon itself and repeats as music often does. The urn characters retell the same tawdry story without being aware that they are repeating themselves. They exist in an endless now where the present and past merge. Similarly, in Silence Ellen is unable to differentiate her youth and old age; the past and present are fused in the image of a twenty-year-old voicing the memories of an old woman. In addition, the endings of Play, Box, Quotations, and both Pinter one-acts suggest circular rather than linear time. In each case, a reprise at play's end repeats lines and themes sounded earlier. The urn characters repeat the entire play; Voice repeats most of her introductory monologue; the trio of Silence repeat many of their lines; and Beth returns to her opening evocation of her man on the beach. Even in Breath, although too brief to include a reprise, the cycle is implied.

Repetition is an important device in the language as well as the structure of dissonant theatre. Whereas in realistic theatre language functions primarily as a container for the play's meanings, in these plays language becomes a spectacle itself.[16] Speech is the primary activity for characters imprisoned in urns or immobile in their chairs. Because visual space is so empty in these plays, bereft of setting and movement, our attention to language is intensified. The poverty of sight heightens the richness of sound. Yet each utterance must overcome enormous physical inertia—speaking becomes a profound act. Both the meaning of the spoken word and the fact of speech are important. Therefore, language is not devalued, as it is in Theatre of the Absurd,[17] but revalued by its new context, measured against the backdrop of physical stasis.

We expect sound to accompany motion—even the motion of the planets was once believed to make the music of the spheres—just as we find silence appropriate to stillness; "still" has complementary meanings of quiet and motionlessness that reveal the implicit connection. But stasis is not accompanied by silence in dissonant drama, but rather by a frenzy of speech, a maelstrom of words. The silence and absence toward which the plays seem to inexorably move never arrive because, paradoxically, the performance demands sound and presence. These plays may be concerned with the absence of community and the silence behind words, but the theatre creates its own de facto community; and a play—if it is a play and not a mime—requires many words. This, then, is the elemental paradox of the theatre of dissonance. It is dramatized by the opposition of the verbal, which creates the community of listeners, and the visual, which suggests that that community is an illusion and that we are essentially isolated from one another. Through the dissonance of sight and sound, Beckett, Albee, and Pinter compel audiences to feel and see their isolation.

Traditional methods of literary dramatic criticism that emphasize the text and exclude the theatrical performance are not sensitive to a theatre based on the separation of sight and sound, because such critical methodologies presume a consonance rather than a dissonance among parts. Ihab Hassan suggests that what we need is "a theory of discontinuity."[18] This study is intended as a modest beginning for such a theory in dramatic criticism.

Like many similar theories of drama, it is what Michael Goodman calls a "polar formula," i.e., composed of paired opposites. This is a natural consequence, Goodman suggests, of the "doubleness of response . . . inherent in the actor-audience encounter."[19] The audience serves as a mirror in which actors judge themselves and their performance according to the audience's response. Through the characters they play, the actors are the audience's alter egos in whom the vicarious experiences of the play are localized. Although this is true of most theatre, the symbiotic relation of actor and audience is further exploited in dissonant drama by two devices: the extensive use of monologue, which heightens our awareness of the actor/character's dependence on the audience; and the shifting of conflict from stage to spectator, which alerts us that the character's behavior is analogous to our own, thereby intensifying the actor-audience bond. This symbiotic relation is suggested explicitly in *Play* by the man's final, desperate question, "Am I as much as . . . being seen?"[20] Some listener, some audience, is a necessary prerequisite to self-definition, as it is to theatre. Ellen echoes the idea in *Silence* when she says, "I must find a person to tell me these things" (*Landscape*, 43). But perhaps Duff's insistence in *Landscape* that Beth enjoys his talking to her, although she gives no signs to suggest this, is the most dramatic illustration of the necessity of some Other—light, lover, silent Minister, spectator—to listen, to watch, and to confer meaning upon our actions.

Actor and audience are united by what Herbert Blau calls "the desire for an extended community."[21] By our presence in the theatre we signal our wish to be part of a larger community. On the stage all these characters, painfully aware of their isolation from one another, speak monologues composed of memories of lovers and loved ones—small extended communities—to silent listeners similar to the theatre audience: the urn characters to the all-seeing light, the Long-Winded Lady to the Minister, Duff to Beth. If these characters were denied an audience, or as in Duff's case even the illusion of an audience, their words would fall unheard, like the tree no one sees or hears falling in the forest.

The performer without an audience is a mere antic. But whoever laughs and cries and applauds an invisible performance is called mad. The theatre of discord gives light and sound to the spectacles our memories perform daily for us in the theatre of the mind.

Notes

Chapter 1. A Theatre of Discord

1. Marshall McLuhan and Quentin Fiore, *The Medium is the Massage* (New York: Bantam, 1967), 57.

2. *Notes and Counter Notes: Writings on the Theatre*, trans. Donald Watson (New York: Grove, 1964), 29.

3. *Beckett: A Study of His Plays* (New York: Hill and Wang, 1972), 110.

4. Samuel Beckett, *Waiting for Godot: A Tragicomedy in Two Acts* (London: Faber and Faber, 1966), 94.

5. *A Theory of Cognitive Dissonance* (Evanston, Ill.: Row, Peterson, 1957), 263.

6. "Cognitive Dissonance in the Plays of Edward Albee," *Quarterly Journal of Speech* 55 (1969): 54–60.

7. Ibid., 57.

8. Ibid., 58 (emphasis added).

9. *Edward Albee: Playwright in Protest* (New York: Avon, 1969), 199.

10. Ibid., 197.

11. Ibid., 189.

12. *Contemporary Drama and the Popular Dramatic Tradition in England* (Totowa, N.J.: Barnes and Noble, 1982), 59–66.

13. Ibid., 61–62.

14. Ibid., 64.

15. *Beckett: A Study of His Plays*, 110.

16. "Beckett's Three Dimensions: Narration, Dialogue, and the Role of the Reader in *Play*," *Modern Drama* 28 (1985): 338.

17. Program note, *Play*, Old Vic, London, 7 April 1964, as quoted in Alec Reid, *All I Can Manage, More Than I Could: An Approach to the Plays of Samuel Beckett* (New York: Grove, 1968), 35.

18. *The Theatre of the Absurd* (Garden City, N.Y.: Anchor-Doubleday, 1969), 5.

19. Ibid., 7 (emphasis added).

20. Ibid., 354.

Chapter 2. The Battle of Lights and Voices: Beckett's *Play* and *Breath*

1. *Play and Two Short Pieces for Radio* (London: Faber, 1964), 9 (emphasis added). Subsequent references are cited by page number in the text.

2. "The Space and the Sound in Beckett's Theatre," in *Beckett the Shape Changer,* ed. Katherine Worth (London: Routledge and Kegan Paul, 1975), 200.

3. Martin Esslin, "Samuel Beckett and the Art of Broadcasting," *Encounter* 45, no. 3 (1975): 44.

4. As quoted in James Knowlson, *Light and Darkness in the Theatre of Samuel Beckett* (London: Turret, 1972), 39.

5. Enoch Brater, "Brecht's Alienated Actor in Beckett's Theatre," *Comparative Drama* 9, no. 3 (1975): 200.

6. *Beckett the Shape Changer,* 185.

7. *Samuel Beckett* (London: Routledge and Kegan Paul, 1976), 90.

8. Bernard F. Dukore, "Beckett's Play, *Play,*" *Educational Theatre Journal* 17, no. 1 (1965): 21.

9. " 'What's it meant to mean?': An Approach to Beckett's Theatre," *Critical Quarterly* 18, no. 2 (1976): 22.

10. Ibid., 23.

11. "Beckett's *Play:* The Circular Line of Existence," *Modern Drama* 18 (1975): 253.

12. *Samuel Beckett: A Critical Study,* 2nd ed. (Berkeley: University of California Press, 1968), 210–211 (emphasis added).

13. " 'What's it meant to mean?' 31.

14. Ibid.

15. *Six Dramatists in Search of a Language: Studies in Dramatic Language* (London: Cambridge University Press, 1975), 231.

16. *Beckett the Shape Changer,* 185.

17. John Fletcher and John Spurling, *Beckett: A Study of His Plays* (New York: Hill and Wang, 1972), 110.

18. Susan Hayward, "The Use of Refrain in Beckett's Plays," *Language and Style* 8, no. 4 (1975): 284.

19. *Samuel Beckett: A Critical Study,* 157.

20. *Beckett: A Study of His Plays,* 107.

21. *Six Dramatists,* 131.

22. Ibid.

23. *Breath and Other Shorts* (London: Faber, 1971), 11.

24. "Being and Non-Being: Samuel Beckett's *Not I,*" *Modern Drama* 19 (1976): 45.

25. *Samuel Beckett* (New York: Viking, 1973), 134.

26. Ibid., 135.

27. "Fool's Progress," in *Samuel Beckett: A Collection of Criticism,* ed. Ruby Cohn (New York: McGraw-Hill, 1975), 35.

28. Deirdre Bair, *Samuel Beckett: A Biography* (New York: Harcourt, 1978), 548.

Chapter 3. The Chinese Box: Albee's *Box* and *Quotations from Chairman Mao Tse-tung*

1. *Box and Quotations from Chairman Mao Tse-tung: Two Inter-related Plays* (New York: Atheneum, 1969), ix. Subsequent references are cited by page number in the text.

2. Michael E. Rutenberg, *Edward Albee: Playwright in Protest* (New York: Avon, 1969), 193.

3. "Albee's Box and Ours," *Modern Drama* 14 (1971): 138.

4. C. W. E. Bigsby, *Albee* (Edinburgh: Oliver & Boyd, 1969), 56.

5. "Conventional Albee: *Box* and *Chairman Mao*," *Modern Drama* 16 (1973), 142.

6. *Six Dramatists in Search of a Language: Studies in Dramatic Language* (London: Cambridge University Press, 1975), 331.

7. Ruby Cohn, *Dialogue in American Drama* (Bloomington: Indiana University Press, 1971), 167.

8. Edward Albee, dir., in touring production of "Albee Directs Albee," Rhode Island College Theatre, Providence, 26 September 1978. The entire piece, *Box and Quotations*, lasted nearly ninety minutes. Description of character movement in *Quotations* is based on this production.

9. *From Tension to Tonic: The Plays of Edward Albee* (Carbondale: S. Illinois University Press, 1972), 124.

10. *Playwright in Protest*, 189.

11. *Edward Albee* (New York: Frederick Ungar, 1973), 124.

12. *Playwright in Protest*, 186.

13. *Who's Afraid of Edward Albee?* (Berkeley: Creative Arts, 1978), 88.

14. Cohn, "Albee's Box," 141; Rutenberg, 188.

15. *Playwright in Protest*, 206, 227.

16. Carol Ann Burns, "Seeing Double: Analogies in the Plays of Edward Albee" (Diss., S.U.N.Y. Binghamton, 1978), 132.

17. *From Tension to Tonic*, 128.

18. "Seeing Double," 140.

19. "*Box* and *Quotations from Chairman Mao Tse-tung*: Albee's Diptych," in *Edward Albee: A Collection of Critical Essays*, ed. C. W. E. Bigsby (Englewood Cliffs, N.J.: Prentice-Hall, 1975), 161.

20. "Conventional Albee," 144.

21. The ellipses in the midst of the Long-Winded Lady's speeches are all part of Albee's text. Nothing has been omitted from her speeches.

22. *Who's Afraid of Edward Albee?*, 88.

23. *Edward Albee*, 124.

24. "The 'Decline of the West' as Reflected in Three Modern Plays," *Educational Theatre Journal* 28, no. 3 (1976): 363–75.

25. *Dialogue*, 165.

26. Allan Wallach, "The LI Interview: Edward Albee," *LI: Newsday's Magazine for Long Island*, 31 December 1978, 18.

27. *Playwright in Protest*, 189.

28. *From Tension to Tonic*, 133.

29. *Edward Albee: A Collection of Critical Essays*, 160.

30. *From Tension to Tonic*, 126.

31. "Existential Valuation in Five Contemporary Plays" (Diss., Bowling Green, 1971), 95.

Chapter 4. Still Life: Pinter's *Landscape* and *Silence*

1. *Box and Quotations from Chairman Mao Tse-tung: Two Inter-related Plays* (New York: Atheneum, 1969), 42.

2. *Landscape and Silence* (New York: Grove, 1970), 7. Subsequent references are cited by page number in the text.

3. *Harold Pinter* (New York: Frederick Ungar, 1973), 123.

4. *The Pinter Problem* (Princeton, N.J.: Princeton University Press, 1975), 231.

5. *The Plays of Harold Pinter: An Assessment* (London: Victor Gallanca, 1973), 154–55. The importance of setting in Pinter's work is further stressed by Steven H. Gale, *Butter's Going Up: A Critical Analysis of Harold Pinter's Work* (Durham, N.C.: Duke University Press, 1977), 177; and by Lucina Paquet Gabbard, *The Dream Structure of Pinter's Plays* (Rutherford, N.J.: Fairleigh Dickinson University Press, 1976), 212.

6. Ibid., 164.

7. *The Pinter Problem*, 241.

8. "Pinter's *Old Times*: The Memory Game," *Modern Drama* 16 (1973): 296n.

9. Ralph Allison and Charles Wellborn, "Rhapsody in an Anechoic Chamber: Pinter's *Landscape*," *Educational Theatre Journal* 25, no. 2 (1973): 215–25, argue that *Landscape*'s "central image, both auditory and visual, is one of contrast between the tenderness or delicacy of the woman's memories of her past and the man's brutal coarseness" (218). Arthur Ganz, "Mixing Memory and Desire: Pinter's Vision in *Landscape*, *Silence* and *Old Times*," in *Pinter: Collection of Essays*, ed. Ganz (Englewood Cliffs, N.J.: Prentice-Hall, 1972), 161–78, says the play is based on the "opposition of force and delicacy, of passion and control" (162). And Simon Trussler sees "two separate modes of being" in the play: "The passive and active, the past and present . . . the woman, dramatically and sexually, complementary to the man" (*The Plays of Harold Pinter*, 159).

10. *Theatre Language: A Study of Arden, Osborne, Pinter and Wesker* (New York: Taplinger, 1972), 95.

11. " 'All These Bits and Pieces': Fragmentation and Choice in Pinter's Plays," *Modern Drama* 17 (1974): 480.

12. *The Pinter Problem*, 57.

13. Ibid., 268.

14. Lois G. Gordon, "Harold Pinter—Past and Present," *Kansas Quarterly* 3, no. 2 (1971): 96.

15. "Déjà Vu: Pinter's 'Silence,' 'Landscape,' 'Silence,' " *Centerpoint* 1, no. 3 (1975): 43.

16. Martin Esslin, *The Peopled Wound: The Work of Harold Pinter* (Garden City, N.Y.: Doubleday, 1970), 195.

17. "Writing for the Theatre," in *Complete Works*, I (New York: Grove, 1976), 14.

18. "Pinter the Spaceman," *Evergreen* no. 55 (1968): 89.

19. *Harold Pinter: The Poetics of Silence* (Carbondale: S. Illinois University Press, 1970), 112.

Chapter 5. Theatre of the Mind

1. "21 Points to the Physicists," in *The Physicists*, trans. James Kirkup (New York: Grove, 1964), 96.

2. *Samuel Beckett: A Biography* (New York: Harcourt, 1978), 523.

3. *Not I*, in *First Love and Other Shorts* (New York: Grove, 1974), 75–87.

4. *Footfalls* (London: Faber, 1976).

5. *That Time* (London: Faber, 1976).

6. Hayman credits Beckett with being "the principal influence" on *Box* and *Quotations* (Albee, 123). Albee confirmed his debt to Beckett in a lecture at the University of Rhode Island, Kingston, R.I., 15 November 1977. Pinter has called Beckett "the most courageous, remorseless writer going and the more he grinds my nose in the shit the more I am grateful to him," in *Beckett at 60: A Festschrift* (London: Calder and Boyars, 1967), 86. And in her biography of Beckett, Bair mentions that Pinter has sent drafts of his plays to Beckett for suggestions (*Samuel Beckett*, 528).

7. *Old Times* (New York: Grove, 1971), 8.

8. "Structure Sonores," in *Sound Sculpture: A Collection of Essays by Artists Surveying the Techniques, Applications and Future Directions of Sound Sculpture*, ed. John Gravson (n.p.: Aesthetic Research Centre of Canada, 1975), 4.

9. *The Theatre of the Absurd* (Garden City, N.Y.: Anchor-Doubleday, 1969), 7.

10. *Proust* (New York: Grove, 1957), 65–66.

11. This is a common comparison, perhaps first promulgated in Ruby Cohn, *Samuel Beckett: The Comic Gamut* (New Brunswick, N.J.: Rutgers University Press, 1962), 237.

12. *Landscape and Silence* (New York: Grove, 1970), 36.

13. *ABC of Reading* (New York: New Directions, 1960), 73.

14. *Dramatic Structure: The Shaping of Experience* (Berkeley: University of California Press, 1970), 137.

15. *The Renaissance: Studies in Art and Poetry* (1910; rpt. New York: Johnson Reprint, 1967), 134, 136.

16. Jean Vannier, "A Theatre of Language," *Tulane Drama Review* 7, no. 3 (1963): 182.

17. *The Theatre of the Absurd*, 7.

18. "Frontiers of Criticism: Metaphors of Silence," in *The Frontiers of Literary Criticism*, ed. David H. Malone (Los Angeles: Hennessey and Ingalls, 1974), 47.

19. *The Actor's Freedom: Toward a Theory of Drama* (New York: Viking, 1975), 17–18.

20. *Play and Two Short Pieces for Radio* (London: Faber, 1964), 22.

21. "Letting Be Be Finale of Seem: The Future of an Illusion," in *Performance in Postmodern Culture*, ed. Michel Benamou and Charles Caramello, Center for Twentieth Century Studies (Madison, Wis.: Coda Press, 1977), 73.

Works Cited

Albee, Edward. *Box and Quotations from Chairman Mao Tse-tung: Two Inter-related Plays.* New York: Atheneum, 1969.

———, dir. *Box and Quotations from Chairman Mao Tse-Tung.* In "Albee Directs Albee," a touring performance of several of Albee's works directed by Albee. Rhode Island College Theatre, Providence. 26 September 1978.

Allison, Ralph, and Charles Wellborn. "Rhapsody in an Anechoic Chamber: Pinter's *Landscape.*" *Educational Theatre Journal* 25, no. 2 (1973): 215–25.

Alvarez, A. *Samuel Beckett.* New York: Viking, 1973.

Avigal, Shoshana. "Beckett's *Play*: The Circular Line of Existence." *Modern Drama* 18 (1975): 251–58.

Bair, Deirdre. *Samuel Beckett: A Biography.* New York: Harcourt, 1978.

Baschet, Bernard. "Structure Sonores." In *Sound Sculpture: A Collection of Essays by Artists Surveying the Techniques, Applications and Future Directions of Sound Sculpture,* edited by John Gravson, 1–12. [Canada]: n.p.: Aesthetic Research Centre of Canada, 1975.

Beckett, Samuel. *Breath and Other Shorts.* London: Faber, 1971.

———. *Footfalls.* London: Faber, 1976.

———. *Not I.* In *First Love and Other Shorts,* 73–87. New York: Grove, 1974.

———. *Play and Two Short Pieces for Radio.* London: Faber, 1964.

———. *Proust.* New York: Grove, 1957.

———. *That Time.* London: Faber, 1976.

———. *Waiting for Godot: A Tragicomedy in Two Acts.* London: Faber, 1966.

Beckett at 60: A Festschrift. London: Calder and Boyars, 1967.

Berry, Jackson G. *Dramatic Structure: The Shaping of Experience.* Berkeley: University of California Press, 1970.

Bigsby, C. W. E. *Albee.* Edinburgh: Oliver and Boyd, 1969.

———. "*Box and Quotations from Chairman Mao Tse-tung*: Albee's Diptych." In *Edward Albee: A Collection of Critical Essays,* edited by C. W. E. Bigsby, 151–64. Englewood Cliffs, N.J.: Prentice-Hall, 1975.

Blau, Herbert. "Letting Be Be Finale of Seem: The Future of an Illusion." In *Performance in Postmodern Culture*, edited by Michel Benamou and Charles Caramello, 59–77. Center for Twentieth Century Studies. Madison, WI: Coda Press, 1977.

Brater, Enoch. "Brecht's Alienated Actor in Beckett's Theatre." *Comparative Drama* 9, no. 3 (1975): 195–205.

Brown, John Russell. *Theatre Language: A Study of Arden, Osborne, Pinter and Wesker.* New York: Taplinger, 1972.

Burns, Carol Ann. "Seeing Double: Analogies in the Plays of Edward Albee." Dissertation, S.U.N.Y. Binghamton, 1978.

Cohn, Ruby. "Albee's Box and Ours." *Modern Drama* 14 (1971): 137–43.

———. *Dialogue in American Drama.* Bloomington: Indiana University Press, 1971.

———. *Samuel Beckett: The Comic Gamut.* New Brunswick, N.J.: Rutgers University Press, 1962.

Davison, Peter. *Contemporary Drama and the Popular Dramatic Tradition in England.* Totowa, N.J.: Barnes and Noble, 1982.

Dukore, Bernard F. "Beckett's Play, *Play.*" *Educational Theatre Journal* 17, no. 1 (1965): 19–23.

Dürrenmatt, Friedrich. "21 Points to the Physicists." In *The Physicists*, trans. by James Kirkup, 96. New York: Grove, 1964.

Esslin, Martin. *The Peopled Wound: The Work of Harold Pinter.* Garden City, N.Y.: Doubleday, 1970.

———. "Samuel Beckett and the Art of Broadcasting." *Encounter* 45, no. 3 (1975): 38–46.

———. *The Theatre of the Absurd.* Garden City, N.Y.: Anchor-Doubleday, 1969.

Festinger, Leon. *A Theory of Cognitive Dissonance.* Evanston, Ill.: Row, Peterson, 1957.

Fletcher, John and John Spurling. *Beckett: A Study of His Plays.* New York: Hill and Wang, 1972.

Gabbard, Lucina Paquet. *The Dream Structure of Pinter's Plays.* Rutherford, N.J.: Fairleigh Dickinson University Press, 1976.

Gale, Steven H. *Butter's Going Up: A Critical Analysis of Harold Pinter's Work.* Durham, N.C.: Duke University Press, 1977.

Ganz, Arthur. "Mixing Memory and Desire: Pinter's Vision in *Landscape, Silence* and *Old Times.*" in *Pinter: Collection of Essays*, edited by Arthur Ganz, 161–78. Englewood Cliffs, N.J.: Prentice-Hall, 1972.

Gillen, Francis. " 'All These Bits and Pieces': Fragmentation and Choice in Pinter's Plays." *Modern Drama* 17 (1974): 477–87.

Goodman, Michael. *The Actor's Freedom: Toward a Theory of Drama.* New York: Viking, 1975.

Gordon, Lois G. "Harold Pinter–Past and Present." *Kansas Quarterly* 3, no. 2 (1971): 89–99.

Hassan, Ihab. "Frontiers of Criticism: Metaphors of Silence." In *The Frontiers of Literary Criticism*, edited by David Malone, 41–47. Los Angeles: Hennessey and Ingalls, 1974.

Hayman, Ronald. *Edward Albee.* New York: Frederick Ungar, 1973.

———. *Harold Pinter.* New York: Frederick Ungar, 1973.

Hayward, Susan. "The Use of Refrain in Beckett's Plays." *Language and Style* 8, no. 4 (1975): 284–92.

Higgens, David. "Existential Valuation in Five Contemporary Plays." Dissertation, Bowling Green, 1971.

Hirsch, Foster. *Who's Afraid of Edward Albee?* Berkeley: Creative Arts, 1978.

Hollis, James R. *Harold Pinter: The Poetics of Silence.* Carbondale: S. Illinois University Press, 1970.

Hopkins, Anthony. "Conventional Albee: *Box* and *Chairman Mao*." *Modern Drama* 16 (1973): 141–47.

Ionesco, Eugène. *Notes and Counter Notes: Writings on the Theatre,* translated by Donald Watson. New York: Grove, 1964.

Kennedy, Andrew. *Six Dramatists in Search of a Language: Studies in Dramatic Language.* London: Cambridge University Press, 1975.

Kenner, Hugh. *Samuel Beckett: A Critical Study,* 2nd ed. Berkeley: University of California Press, 1968.

Knowlson, James. *Light and Darkness in the Theatre of Samuel Beckett.* London: Turret, 1972.

Lahr, John. "Pinter the Spaceman." *Evergreen,* no. 55 (1968): 49–52, 87–90.

Laughlin, Karen. "Beckett's Three Dimensions: Narration, Dialogue, and Role of the Reader in *Play*." *Modern Drama* 28 (1985): 338.

Martineau, Stephen. "Pinter's *Old Times*: The Memory Game." *Modern Drama* 16 (1973): 287–97.

McLuhan, Marshall and Quentin Fiore. *The Medium is the Massage.* New York: Bantam, 1967.

Mullin, Donald. "The 'Decline of the West' as Reflected in Three Modern Plays." *Educational Theatre Journal* 28, no. 3 (1976): 363–75.

Paolucci, Anne. *From Tension to Tonic: The Plays of Edward Albee.* Carbondale: S. Illinois University Press, 1972.

Pater, Walter. *The Renaissance: Studies in Art and Poetry.* 1910; rpt. New York: Johnson Reprint, 1967.

Pilling, John. *Samuel Beckett.* London: Routledge and Kegan Paul, 1976.

Pinter, Harold. *Landscape and Silence*. New York: Grove, 1970.

————. *Old Times*. New York: Grove, 1971.

————. "Writing for the Theatre." In *Complete Works*, vol. I, 9–16. New York: Grove, 1976.

Post, Robert M. "Cognitive Dissonance in the Plays of Edward Albee." *Quarterly Journal of Speech* 55 (1969): 54–60.

Pound, Ezra. *ABC of Reading*. New York: New Directions, 1960.

Quigley, Austin E. *The Pinter Problem*. Princeton, N.J.: Princeton University Press, 1975.

Reid, Alec. *All I Can Manage, More Than I Could: An Approach to the Plays of Samuel Beckett*. New York: Grove, 1968.

Rutenberg, Michael E. *Edward Albee: Playwright in Protest*. New York: Avon, 1969.

Takahashi, Yasanuri. "Fool's Progress." In *Samuel Beckett: A Collection of Criticism*, edited by Ruby Cohn, 33–40. New York: McGraw-Hill, 1975.

Trussler, Simon. *The Plays of Harold Pinter: An Assessment*. London: Victor Gallancz, 1973.

Vannier, Jean. "A Theatre of Language." *Tulane Drama Review* 7, no. 3 (1963): 180–86.

Wallach, Allan. "The LI Interview: Edward Albee." *LI: Newsday's Magazine for Long Island* 31 December 1978: 17–18, 24, 27, 30.

Whittemore, Nena T. "Déjà Vu: Pinter's 'Silence,' 'Landscape,' 'Silence.'" *Centerpoint* 1, no. 3 (1975): 41–46.

Wilcher, Robert. "'What's it meant to mean?': An Approach to Beckett's Theatre." *Critical Quarterly* 18, no. 2 (1976): 9–37.

Worth, Katherine. "The Space and the Sound in Beckett's Theatre." In *Beckett the Shape Changer*, edited by Katherine Worth, 185–218. London: Routledge and Kegan Paul, 1975.

Zeifman, Hersch. "Being and Non-Being: Samuel Beckett's *Not I*." *Modern Drama* 19 (1976): 35–46.

Index

Albee, Edward, 34–51; his admiration for Beckett, 70; box as common symbol of, 34–35; compared to Beckett, 49; as director of *Box* and *Quotations*, 39, 43; dramatic form altered by, 49; grandmother characters of, 42–43; guarded optimism of, 50; inward journey of, compared to Beckett's, 72; mental processes in works of, 73; on playwright's obligations, 49; on role of artist, 50, 51; and theatre of discord, 14, 19, 70; and Theatre of the Absurd, 18; Voice as surrogate for, 50; warning to civilization by, 50

All Over: box as symbol in, 34

Alvarez, A.: on *Breath*, 31–32

American Dream, The: box as symbol in, 34; compared to *Quotations*, 43

Audience: analogous relation of, to actor/characters, 26, 75; analogous relation of, to spotlight in *Play*, 26–27; as co-producers of meaning, 19; expectations of, 14, 47; as protagonists, 18, 69; and struggle to resolve dissonance, 15, 16, 54, 64. *See also* Theatre of discord

Audience's role: in *Box*, 36, 50; in *Landscape*, 54, 67, 75; in *Play*, 26–27; in *Quotations*, 49, 50; in *Silence*, 64, 67, 75. *See also* Theatre of discord

Avigal, Shoshana: on *Play*, 27

Baschet, Bernard: on role of artist, 72

Beckett, Samuel, 20–33; admired by Albee and Pinter, 70; compared to Albee, 49; critics of, 17; as director of *Play*, 30; later dissonant plays by, 70; light vs. language in works of, 70; mental processes in works of, 73; on "the mess," 69; new dramatic form sought by, 69–70; optimism in language of, 32; on struggle facing contemporary artist, 69; and theatre of discord, 14, 19, 70; and Theatre of the Absurd, 18

Berry, Jackson G.: on dramatic structure, 73

Bigsby, C. W. E.: on *Quotations*, 41, 49

Blau, Herbert: on actor/audience desire for community, 75

Box, 14, 35–38; audience's role in, 36, 50; compared to *Landscape* and *Silence*, 62, 67; conflict between light and language in, 37; conflict relocated to audience in, 36; dissonance in, 14–16, 37; enmeshed with *Quotations*, 34; image of birds in, 37; images of loss in, 36; as metaphor, 35; reprise of, compared to *Silence*, 67; role of voice in, 35; setting of, 35; theme of civilization's decline in, 36, 50; verbal vs. visual in, 35

Breath, 14, 31–33; brevity of, 31; compared to *Box* and *Quotations*, 49; compared to *Play*, 32–33, 34; dissonance in, 32, 33; human condition in, 31; human sound as metaphor in, 32; inspiration in, 31, 32; light as metaphor in, 31, 32; pessimistic interpretation of, 33; rhythms of life and death in, 32; unresolved tension of, 33

Brown, John Russell: on *Landscape*, 60

Cognitive dissonance. *See* Dissonance

Cohn, Ruby: on *Box* and *Quotations*, 34, 49

Davison, Peter: on *Landscape* and *Silence*, 17